The Literature of Fact

The Literature of Fact

SELECTED PAPERS FROM THE ENGLISH INSTITUTE

EDITED WITH A FOREWORD BY ANGUS FLETCHER

NEW YORK

Columbia University Press

1976

Library of Congress Cataloging in Publication Data
English Institute.
    The literature of fact.

    Papers from two sessions of the English Institute,
held in 1974 and 1975.
    Includes bibliographical references.
    1. Literature and history—Addresses, essays,
lectures.   I. Fletcher, Angus John Stewart, 1930—   II. Title.
PN50.E5   1976   809   76-25582
ISBN 0-231-04144-6

Columbia University Press
New York—Guildford, Surrey

IN MEMORIAM

❧⚜❧

Reuben A. Brower
and
William K. Wimsatt

❦

Foreword

The "Literature of Fact" occupied the attention of the English Institute during two sessions of its meetings, in 1974 and 1975. Professor E. D. Hirsch envisioned and organized the first session, with papers by Robert Nisbet, David Fischer, and Paul Fussell. The present editor organized a second series for 1975. Professor Hirsch held that literary scholars could usefully analyze the interaction of "literature" and "fact," since to consider the status of fact in literature meant to reconsider basic questions about value and the critical evaluation of literary efforts. The rubric was especially enticing because, although it might lead to pseudo-statements about both its terms, these terms would still remind us that the facts of science and experience appear to be formally antithetical to poetic figuration, to poetic image, to poetic vision. At the same time it seems clear that literary imagination is always somehow connected with reality; that is, literature can hardly be disconnected from fact. If schizophrenia defines complete disconnection from fact, then strong and natural connection is defined by the literary modes of memoir, history and case history, scientific *compte rendu,* analytic discourse in the social and natural sciences, in short by all the discursive literary modes. We are only beginning to understand the linkages between documents and legends, data and models, facts and fictions. The English Institute panelists joined in suggesting that we need to consider these linkages more closely.

For the student of literature one clear emphasis emerged from the Literature of Fact essays. All three papers for 1974 tended to dwell upon history and historiography, with their ancilla, the social sciences. Professor Nisbet observed that Cartesian influences upon the social sciences ran counter to the Baconian insistence upon discovery, as opposed to demonstration. Fussell, whose paper has since appeared in his book *The Great War and Modern Memory,* raised questions about "factual" literary form, focussing on the "non-fictional or sub-fictional" genre of the memoir. This genre particularly interests Fussell in that it is difficult to distinguish from the "first novel" of the young author (and how young were the victims, living and dead, of the Great War!), since the youthful author seems destined to use his own life story as the basis of his plot. Fussell concluded with

the sobering thought that memoirs of the kind I have been focussing on here have been used as fundamental materials for the writing of history. We may be led to the conclusion that there can be no history; there can be only literary history. Our access to events, even so significant an event as the Great War, must be through the makers of plots—that, is, poets. As one critic has observed recently, "Our evidence [for history] is itself verbal; a document, a memoir, a charter are semantic acts whose correspondence with actuality, whose 'truth-function,' is no greater than that of other verbal modes." Our predicament as imaginations suspended between fact and art, prevented by each from wholly understanding the other, is implied with perhaps a deceptive levity by

Wilde in *The Critic as Artist:* the well-named Ernest asks, "Life, then, is a failure?" To which Gilbert answers: "From the artistic point of view, certainly."

Today the critic as artist may wish to deal with the suspension between fact and art as an uncertain suspension between memorandum and memoir, but if he is to work somewhat less aesthetically and somewhat more systematically with the idea of imagination encountering documentary materials, he must enter the difficult fields of epistemology, perception, and the psychology of aesthetic creation—the last a field of almost total obscurity at the present time. If the critic wants to explain the relation between poetic artifice (plots, image clusters, archetypes, poetic rhythms, and the like) and the "truth" of documentary materials, then he must analyze his canons of evidence, as a scientist would. I regret that, in the light of my last remark, none of the papers in the Literature of Fact section dealt with one of the most critical fact / fiction dilemmas, the introduction of legal thought into imaginative literary works. For the law plays back and forth between facts of cases and broad interpretive legal concepts. Furthermore, the law (witness Vico's anthropological "mythistoria") has developed into one of the most powerful and persistent modes of verbal and cultural tradition in the West, so that its study amounts to a study of the twinned coexistence of fact and idea, as these bear upon the continuing "artistic failure" of our lives.

History, however, remains the largest domain to be set off against imaginative literature. Aristotle held, in the *Poetics*, that history was less philosophical than poetry, because it was tied to the truth of particulars. Poetry, built up from a fundamentally mythic ground, is philosophical, because its myths are recurrent, enduring forms—ideas in motion. To the extent that poetry could free itself from the infinite particularity of history, as the drama could do, by compressing narrative into pure theatrical action, it attained a greater and more exact degree of philosophical truth. (The novel, not yet existing, is not, for Aristotle, a problem.) Aristotle believed the drama capable of a clarity of line impossible in the comprehensive epic form. The drama reached ideality, the more it removed itself from the particularities that make epic so splendidly full. Drama, seen thus, clarifies the relation of fact to fiction by removing itself as far as possible, through a contraction of its mythic scale, from the expanding and discursive anthropological layout of the epic poem. Since, for late classic Greek culture, Homeric epic was formally entangled with the historiography of Herodotus as well as the more modern Thucydides, the dramatist's excisions of fact are a strategic move of great philosophic intuition. We still live with the problem of dramatized versus narrated action, as the Literature of Fact papers amply testify.

All papers included in the present volume deal with narrative expression of one sort or another. At least two papers, those of Turner and Mazzaro, deal with dramatic aspects of narrative. Our scholars have gone back to the riddle which preceded and elicited the Aristotelian dictum regarding the superiority of drama over epic. In various ways our essays deal with story, whether in *mythos* or *historia* (the Herodotean word meaning "researches") or dramatic *praxis*. As usually happens with Institute papers, the ensuing essays were composed in complete independence of one another. All the more striking, then, that they all focus on analogous questions about the nature of narrative discourse. The reader will notice many striking recurrences of ideas from one paper to the next. For example, both Frye and Said deal with memory, with revolution, with representation, with empire, with the idea that "history repeats itself," while Hayden White joins Frye (whose theory of archetypes informed White's theoretical study of historiography, *Metahistory*) in dealing with modes of "higher" and "lower" criticism, to mention only one conjunction between the two authors. Similar sharings of concern will appear throughout the collection.

Whatever common ground is shared by the six papers on the Literature of Fact, each one has its characteristic stance which differentiates it from the others. Frye assumes that the most influential of all "historical" visions in the West, the Bible, speaks the "primary language" of literature. The Bible is seen to be the most complex of all literary artifacts. Yet this view does not yield a "Bible as literature"—a classic text for exclusively aesthetic response and judgment—it becomes "a practically untapped source of self-transforming power." Frye confronts us with a deep paradox. He does *not* want the reader to regard the Bible "as a seamless web of myth and metaphor"—which those who misread Frye would expect him to want. Instead, he observes that "if we want to go from the imaginative to the existential, we have to try to take a step forward from our literary understanding, in the opposite direction from the historical." We are to rest neither in the arms of metaphor and myth nor in the embrace of history. We have rather to regard Biblical narrative and prophecy as a system of monadic symbols, what medieval interpreters would have called an anagogic mirror of reality. Thus Frye concludes that "the real step forward comes when we see that the entire Biblical vision, from Genesis to Revelation (or Chronicles in Judaism), may be spiritually present in every particular event, and may be in fact the genuine form of that event." Our own lives provide the testing ground for this anagogic, monadic vision. Events become instances of a concrete universal, in the Hegelian phrase, or Leibnitzian monads or the exegete's anagogy, because a providential meaning inheres in the ephemera of human life, as long as these ephemera are tested against the long-term vision of the literary form of the Bible. Frye, in short, views human history and myth from the point of view of revelation in general and also in the particular context of the Book of Revelation. His essay provides a general framework for the student of Hebraic-Christian myth and history.

Because the other essayists are perhaps more modest in their ambitions, their main interests can be more easily epitomized. Hayden White here pursues an inquiry which he opened up on a broad basis in his *Metahistory,* a massive study of the poetic figuration of historical writing. White has shown that some historians lean toward one major figure of speech, e.g., synecdoche, while others lean toward another, e.g., irony. In the present essay White shows that the figural approach to historiography allows us to "construe" the fields of data and interpretation represented by major historical narratives. White refuses to believe that the choice of data to be historically recounted is ever neutral; it is always subject to prefigurational bias and tendency; the historian always opts for one governing trope or another. When White analyzes Darwinian narrative in some detail, he is able to show that Darwin's scientific imperatives lead him naturally to a preference for the figure of metonymy. White, in short, here presents a test case for the theory of the troping of historical discourse and narrative.

Victor Turner alerts the reader to another major problem in the Literature of Fact, the necessity to compare, not merely one kind of mythic or narrative from with some other such form, but also to compare the synchronic rise of analogous forms in quite different, even opposed, cultural contexts. Turner gives us an elaborated case study for comparative analysis, pitting an African ritual drama of affliction against the highly sophisticated literary mixture of myth and history constituted by the *Purgatorio* of Dante. Turner is able to make his comparison work, because he employs the underlying concept of "processual form," a concept equally applicable to both his main instances. As an anthropologist, Turner is at home in structural comparisons of symbolic forms, and because his interests are deeply literary, he goes beyond Lévi-Straussian, Saussurian structuralism, into a broader field of semiotic conjecture. If Frye and most of the other contributors extend our awareness of the diachronic dimension of myth and history, Turner reminds us of the need to make synchronic comparisons between different cultural sets. Broadly, he introduces the anthropologist's concerns into the field of literary fact.

Mazzaro deepens this concern, with a close reading of the most concentrated of all historiographic forms, the autobiography. His example, *The Vita Nuova,* stands effectively at the beginning of a major post-classical tradition. As is so often the case with great originators, Dante creates in Beatrice a figure not only dramatically dominant in "her" fiction, but also complex and multiform in her symbolic implications. Mazzaro takes *The Vita Nuova* out of the overly simple exegetic context of the poetry of courtly love, with its "romantic screens" standing between "Beatrice" and "the poet." Mazzaro emphasizes the more powerful symbolic modes of mediation that come into play when the fiction is given theological valences. Dante's Beatrice then is shown to help generate a literary tradition of numinous autobiography, whose transformations Mazzaro follows in the work of autobiographic poets like Petrarch, Sidney, and Wordsworth. Mazzaro's contribution can best be understood as an analysis of the underlying structures of autobiographic sequence, that is, of the literary forms required by the projection of a personal, self-known "self," whose ultimate problem is to separate the developing, autobiographical personality from the surrounding pressures of a culture-bound other. Mazzaro shares anthropological concerns with Turner, and it seems critical that both write about Dante.

David Fischer presents a gentle polemic. He argues for the historian's need to write a "braided narrative," a story line allowed to be sufficiently complex in both action and decor, such that three major historiographic requirements are met. Particularly in the field of social history these three requirements arise from Fischer's belief that his field comprises both an art *and* a science. This double nature demands (a) that the historian develop new forms of narration, (b) that he develop new techniques of characterization for the presentation of his *dramatis personae,* and (c) that he refine the fact-finding apparatus of scholarship. Fischer's emphasis on American historians gives his

paper a special relevance to the student of imaginative literature, since it has been shown, by David Levin and others, that
American historiography has strong romantic tendencies, in line
with a deep cultural bias in American life from Colonial times
to the present. Fischer gives us a variety of analytic perspectives.
With other writers in this symposium he stresses the role of the
paradigm for narrative. In this way he is able to suggest the
outlines of a theory of historiographic *action,* as distinct from
White's demonstration of a theory of historiographic *figuration.*

Finally, Edward Said attacks the question of fact in myth and
history, particularly the latter, by asking about supposed
"facts," Are they genuine? Vico is shown to develop a theory or
quasi-theory of the link between historical causation and historical descent. At some length Said reminds us of the way Vico
traces the meanings of the term "gentile," a term pointing to
the concept of generation and implying systems of genealogy.
What is true, historically, in Vico, is whatever descends to us
with gentile significance (the term is effectively denuded of its
Jew / Gentile, polarizing sense). Said then distinguishes between history as the narrative of essentially biological descent
("filiation") and history as the narrative of non-natural descent
("affiliation"). Said's example is the historical myth of the paternity of Louis Napoleon. This example permits Said to show that
the order and power of affiliations, rather than direct filiations,
confer the status of fact upon Napoleonic history. Said demon-
strates that man the historian can create his present and his
genealogical past (in the broadest sense) by completely
disregarding the facts of nature; Louis Napoleon can pretend
that he is the direct descendant, rather than what he actually

was, the nephew of Napoleon Bonaparte. By advancing upon certain insights of Marx, Said is able to show that the facts of affiliation may be every bit as powerful, rhetorically and politically, as the facts of direct filiation. Said's essay analyzes a well-known abuse of history, the "big lie." In effect, "On Repetition" discloses the nature of propaganda. It shows how propagandists exploit facts, spreading them about in various affiliative fictions. Said goes to the heart of our problem and substitutes for Frye's synthesizing method his own analytic method, centered on the filiation / affiliation dialectic.

The reader will have noticed that, given a certain amount of circling around and about a broad and scarcely definable main topic, the order of papers had inevitably to be circular. Thus, at the widest edges of the Literature of Fact both Frye and Said discuss the origination of myths and histories; both authors treat of self-contained cultural traditions and their means of transmitting values from one generation to the next. A concentricity of interest joins Frye and Said in their treatment of mythic and historiographic origins. Frye shows that for the Jews and Christians of the Biblical world all legitimate history has to be authorized by an ultimate reliance on the truth of a genetic, Genesis-myth, with its metaphysical *con-sequence.* Said shows that for the filiative myth of an imperial "Napoleonic order" there had to be an affiliative embedding of that myth in the pseudo-facts of revolutionary and counter-revolutionary rhetorical warfare. Frye and Said equally stress the emergence of imaginative fictions during prolonged periods of revolutionary change; they are equally aware that great imagination draws also on the repetitions of events as seen by poets and storytellers of more conservative periods. Frye ends his essay with a tentative assertion, Said with a positive question. The two essays complement each other, defining the central issues and the outer limits of our topic.

By setting White and Fischer off against each other, we find a similar concentricity. White argues for the necessary figuration of historical narratives, Fischer for the need to subject this figuration to the demands of untropable historical facts. Both White and Fischer are aware that many of the facts "won't fit." To show how a great historical mind, Darwin, meets this difficulty, White analyzes what happens when Darwin introduces time into the taxonomic description of natural history, while Fischer treats various ways in which the social historian forms the chaotic mass of material available from private memoirs, government statistics, and so on. The two papers will interest the student of figurative language because they demonstrate, in different cases, the scientific need to employ metonymy. If Darwin decorates his taxonomically-ordered "history" of evolution with metonymic figures, and if the social historian employs Fischer's ideal metonymic footnote and statistical excursus, there would appear to be a necessary parallel between the social historian and the evolutionary theorist. White and Fischer are certainly aware of each other's theoretical problems, and for this reason it seems no accident that, taken together, the essays of White and Fischer comprise a rather full account of the varied field of historiographic forms.

The middle ground of this collection is provided by two essays that focus on a reading of Dante. Turner and Mazzaro (the latter's paper being the only one not delivered before the

Institute audience) give us a more detailed commentary than the
other authors found it convenient to provide. Turner recounts
not only a story of anthropological data-gathering as a format
for research, but tells this as his own Herodotean *historia*. We
learn exactly how he came into the teaching of Dante and the
experiencing of an alien cultural life in his own fieldwork,
which he likens, significantly, to the primal experience of "first
love" (one more analogue to Fussell's "first novel" paradigm?).
Mazzaro recounts the "history" of Dante's famed epiphanic encounter with the visionary Beatrice Portinari, an encounter
forming the basis, first for *The Vita Nuova* and later for *The
Divine Comedy*. An interest in affliction and comedy gives power
as well as shape to both Turner's and Mazzaro's essays. The ex-
pository detail in each paper is systematically required, for there
can be no adequate treatment of Dante for English-speaking
readers without an accounting of what most strikes us, i.e., the
extremely detailed, factified, poetry of "the secular world" (in
Auerbach's phrase) of Dante's poetic vision. The two central
papers manifestly provide a more densely articulated me-
talinguistic context than their flanking outriders. Students of
literature may wonder at first at the plethora of anthropological
data given by Turner, whose first studies, it should be said,
were in the literary field. But this fullness arises naturally from
the anthropologist's need to show that fact / fiction relations can
only be focused if the critical eye opens to an *extensive* variety of
experiential details in the life of the culture to be explored, be it
a tribal ritual or a highly sophisticated literary artifact such as
The Divine Comedy. The student of epic must take in a manifold
of many cultural attitudes. I am particularly happy to be able to

include Turner's discussion of the *Purgatorio*—a vision of innumerable thresholds—since in a number of books, including *The Ritual Process,* he has developed theories of initiatory liminality for the study of literature and life. His work will help the student of ritual drama; it is immediately germane to the analysis of epic quest-forms. Mazzaro, by the same token, deals with the intricate theological and epistemological bases for the "realization" of Dante's Beatrice (his *Transformations in the Renaissance English Lyric,* Cornell, 1970, has a chapter on *"Res-Verba* Relations"); Beatrice was utterly real, present and physical for Dante, but she was at the same time utterly unreal and visionary, as she appears in his poems. Mazzaro, I think rightly, gives the Virgilian Dante the pride of place in the literary tradition of autobiographical fiction. Like Turner, with his emphasis on tribal filiation and cultural affiliation (a topic stressed for later authors by Said), and with his emphasis on the specific liminal format of *communitas,* Mazzaro (pp. 95 ff.) deals with the levels of community invoked by the Dantesque vision of Beatrice and her social and spiritual "class." What issues clearly from these two central discussions is the idea that if poets are to gain maximum visionary force in the era of post-classical literature, they must simultaneously put greatest pressure on numinous vision (Beatrice the spiritual Being) and on historically-known, confining fact (Beatrice the child of real parents, the object of real desire on the part of Dante the real man, who was born, lived, and died, with the accepted, documented dates, 1265-1321 A.D.). The poet must do so, because only in memory is there the fullness of time. Mazzaro further broaches the question of the relation between a memorious fiction, such as *The Vita*

Nuova, and the revolutionary, future-oriented prophetic modality
of literature.

While the six papers included in this symposium are arranged
concentrically, their circles in addition advance from a more or
less settled interest in myth, metaphor, and ritual (Frye, White,
and Turner) to an increasing concentration on unadulterated historical fact in the final three papers. Yet this tendency to weight
the historical as primary emerges only slowly in the course of
the volume. With Fischer and Said we are at last quite fully inside the domain of the historiographer's mode of symbolic action. This emerging focus may be an artifact of my own selec-
tive process, but if so, I hope it accords with present interests.

One great issue in contemporary literary scholarship is the ad-
justment of the complementary, but formally different claims of
mythography and historiography, of myth criticism and theory
of history. As the ensuing essays suggest in various ways, history is undercutting the mythic apprehension of reality at the
present time. Because in their different ways all of the essays in
this volume acknowledge this conflict, they all interconnect and
play to each other.

This ludic arrangement makes the emergence of a history-
oriented stress all the more crucial, since historical (or social-
anthropological) facts disrupt the regular recurrences of archetype and myth. The unexpected, the emergent, the aleatory
event—these confuse the myths and metaphors our tradition has
always used when it wants to make sense of life by showing its
recurrent patternings. It is always a question: which is more
ominous, something new, or something old, something strange,
or something familiar? It is a question: must revelation always

be, as the old German Bible has it, a *heimlich* or uncanny revelation? We seem to have entered an Age of Uncanny Questions, a
postlude to the Ages of the Enlightenment and Romanticism.
Our questions are ominous, as in earlier ages of sensibility. If
we face the past in our literary activities, we must confront anx-
ieties of influence. Yet we remain only half daunted by our ancestors. We continue to look ahead as well, and thus we meet
the fact of the history of Western culture, that it long ago
marked out a collision course, to bring fact and idea into impossible union. It was with this large historical catachresis in mind
that the Literature of Fact section was put together.

Perhaps the most striking consensus solicited by the six
papers would be the belief that as one moves from the sacred to
the secular one is forced to accept a greater and greater degree of
heterogeneity of factual materials considered by authors to be
relevant to their discourse. Thus Frye is enabled to advance authoritative, homogeneous myth to a privileged position in the
construction of the Bible. Thus White is enabled to emphasize
figurative language in the natural history of Darwin, owing, it
would appear, to the fact that as one critic said, Natural Selection was functioning for Darwin as a kind of progressive goddess. Darwin remains critical, because his work is in every other
sense a "scientific" activity, not a rhetorical game. Yet a sacred
rhetoric contaminates Darwin's discourse. Similar contami-
nations occur in Dante's epic anthropology and personal myth-
making, as Turner and Mazzaro show. (Frye has recently identified romance as a "secular scripture.") Further along the scale,
as legend takes up the burden of straight historiography, Fischer
and Said both show that the historian and the maker of history

have to include details of fact which prevent mythic homogene-
ity from taking over the narrative. Fischer helpfully gives us a
broad perspective on the present-day situation of the social historian, who is separated by at least four generations from the
time when historiography could still confidently make its pro-
tagonists into heroes, its great stories into quasi-mythic accounts of heroic deeds. In stressing the corporateness of historical activity, Fischer gives space to the free play of heterogeneous
historical events; he therefore wants to develop a rhetoric of the
ancillary detail, through a skilled deployment of the "note" and
the statistical array. He refuses to cut out these apparently
diversionary materials simply on the ground that they get in the
way of a smooth narrative order. To encourage the social historian of today, Fischer cites the masterful example of Gibbon.

The heterogeneous plenitude of history, its "plethoric" character (Michel Foucault's term), have long been a problem for
masters of this type of fact-oriented literature. Herodotus made
factual plenitude the underlying basis for his deep relativism in
regard to truth values: "For myself, my duty is to report all that
is said, but I am not obliged to believe it all alike—a remark
which may be understood to apply to my whole History" (*The
Persian Wars*, VII, 152). When, with the rise of positivism, historians came to believe that they could really discover all the
main facts, they were even more deeply committed to reporting
the plethora of history—from an antiHerodotean point of view.
In short, history may be understood to be that literary mode
most deeply committed to endless expansion of its materials
through discourse; history, in short, is what Arnold van Gen-
nep, in *The Semi-Scholars*, amusingly called "the endless research project." History must therefore comprise the domain

where "facts" are most numerous, and the historiographic process is seen to be inherently accumulative and without terminus, somewhat as if it were the narrative of a journey backward into a regressively expanding universe.

At the same time, human mortality being what it is, historians counter their own tendency toward heterogeneous expansion. They do this through the arbitrary imposition of form, or idea. By noting this imposition, we may escape the banal trouble that arises if we imagine literature and fact to be destructively opposed to each other. What is spoken or written may be factual or not, as the interpreter chooses. The critical opposition lies elsewhere, as will be seen if we make one slight alteration in a passage from Lionel Trilling's essay "The Meaning of a Literary Idea." This essay in *The Liberal Imagination* started from a basic observation "that literature is of its nature involved with ideas because it deals with man in society, which is to say that it deals with formulations, valuations, and decisions, some of them implicit, others explicit." This sentence could be entirely reoriented, by the simple substitution of "facts" for "ideas," without in any obvious way being falsified. Our formulations, valuations, and decisions equally involve our sense of fact. That this substitution of "fact" and "idea" is at least not absurd indicates that facts have no meaning until they are given form, or ideal order. The Literature of Fact, whatever its area of expression, is then a literature placing ideal pressures, pressures from the standpoint of theory, upon the lumpen heterogeneity of fact. As the present collection of papers shows, we can demonstrate different types and periods of ideological and ideational pressure upon unformed fact.

The literary imagination is forever being reborn, so that we

need not lament such supposed calamities as the demise of the
novel, that most factful and tactful of genres. The novel has already transformed itself, toward biography, the non-fiction
novel, the kabbalistic novel of Pynchon. Fisher's example of
Cochrane's Florentine *History* points to complementary moves
made in the field of historiography. Writers, in short, will rise
to meet the occasion of our flood of incoming data. In this
regard there is a peculiarly tantalizing prospect open to criticism: the development beyond Kenneth Burke of a "rhetoric of
fact," a rhetorical analysis of the ways "the facts," as newspaper-
men call them, may be deployed with far greater rhetorical
power than ever could the fine figures of speech drawn from
classical models. Today the pretence of fact is figuratively more
powerful than the pretence of figuration. That poetry *was* most
true which *was* most feigning; today that poetry is most true
which is least feigning. Since we live in a documentary age, we
have to think about our relation to documents. In this sense we
are committed, afflicted, and caught by, the Literature of Fact.

City University of New York   ANGUS FLETCHER
March, 1976

Contents

The Literature of Fact

~§§~

History and Myth in the Bible

We should expect to find the greatest imaginative powers among oppressed peoples. Strong and successful nations, like ancient Rome, Edwardian Britain, or contemporary America and Russia, tend to be somewhat earth-bound in their cultural products and to keep their real imaginative exuberance for their engineering. The intensity of Biblical vision has much to do with the fact that the Hebrews were never lucky at the game of empire. The Bible records only two periods of relative prosperity for Israel: the period of David and Solomon and the period following the Maccabean rebellion, and the reason was much the same in both cases: one world empire had declined and its successor had not yet arisen. This link between imaginative intensity and alienation is not confined to the Hebrews: in medieval Europe there seems to be a distinctive kind of creative energy among the Celtic tribes squeezed into the remote corners of Western Europe. The Arthurian legends might well have become, in a different cultural setting, the starting point of great apocalyptic visions of Celtic triumph and Teutonic or Latin disaster, paralleling the Biblical dreams of a fallen Babylon and an eternal Jerusalem. Even Yeats, writing in a Teutonic language, still finds enough vitality in Cuchulain and Oisin to think of them as part of a mythology that may be remembered in a future that has forgotten Christ. Yeats had, Eliot says, a "minor mythology," but so did the Biblical prophets and apostles on the periphery of the Roman world.

Religious structures tend to expand as their societies expand. Small communities live in a world in which most of the gods are local and epiphanic ones, the ancestors of the nymphs and fauns and fairies of a later age. Larger social units, big enough to have aristocracies, produce a set of departmental and administrative gods on the analogy of such aristocracies. The larger the social organization, the further the gods retreat, from trees and rivers to mountain-tops, from mountain-tops into the sky. When large nations become empires, whose rulers begin to think of themselves as rulers of the world, the notion of monotheism takes shape. Monotheism appeared in Egypt before the Biblical period, and more continuously in Persia and the later Classical world. This is imperial monotheism, in which the ruler normally is the representative, sometimes the actual incarnation, of one supreme god. Such a monotheism is tolerant of local cults, but expands into a sense of the order of nature, particularly the heavenly bodies, as the visible counterpart of the one invisible God. The most impressive form of this monotheism in history, probably, was the Stoicism expounded by Posidonius, which is reflected in a good deal of Manilius, Cicero, and Virgil.

We can hardly overestimate the importance, for our own cultural tradition, of the fact that Biblical monotheism, the basis of Judaism, Christianity, and Islam, is a revolutionary movement, totally different in social context and reference from imperial monotheism. The story of Israel begins with God in the burning bush, informing Moses that he is giving himself a spe-

his narrative there is no boundary line anywhere clearly
that separates myth from legend, legend from historical
scence, reminiscence from didactic history, didactic from
history. The Bible, considered as history, is a baffling and
ating document which the historian has to learn how to
d it creates more problems than it solves. The inference
interested in at the moment is: if there is anything in the
vhich is historically accurate, it is not there because it is
ally accurate, but for quite different reasons. The reasons
involve what we may call spiritual significance. Histori-
racy has no relation to spiritual significance, unless per-
e relation is an inverse one. The spiritual significance of
k of Job, which nobody has ever thought of as anything
an imaginative drama, is obviously greater than the lists
es in the Book of Chronicles, which may well contain au-
records.

g aware of history and being historical are different
A hundred years ago, critics of Homer were inclined to
ze the historical basis of the Trojan War and assume that
t made it up out of his own head. Schliemann began to
some archaeological evidence (of a very equivocal kind,
be said) that there was a city more or less where Homer
vas, and since then scholars have acquired a considerable
for Homer's sense of fact, in both history and geogra-
ut no increasing respect for such matters will make
' fight with the river-god or the hurling of Hephaistos
eaven less mythical: those are as mythical as ever, and
ss always will be. More simply, Homer's sense of history
t mean that he is writing history. Similarly with the

cific name and is about to enter history in a highly partisan role,
taking the side of an oppressed people against their overlords.
There even seems to be some evidence that the word "Hebrew"
itself, back in Abraham's time, originally meant something
more like "proletariat" than a conventional name for a people.
Two features of a revolutionary mind are particularly important
for us here. First, it is a dialectical and polarizing mind: whatever is not for it is against it, and it seeks to reduce or eliminate
all middle ground, all liberal, eclectic, or "revisionist" attitudes. God consistently speaks of himself as "jealous," intolerant of any deviation in ritual or doctrine. Many gods are not different aspects of him: they are his enemies: like an earthly ruler,
he can tolerate only subordinates. Second, a revolutionary mind
is intensely concentrated on a reversal of the social order which
is bound to occur in the future, a future which may be simply
future time, or, as in apocalyptic literature, the end of time,
but which is made, in the writer's expectations, as near and as
imminent as he can get it.

Imperial monotheism reflects a strong and secure human
order that feels able to come to terms with the order of nature.
It expresses itself in visual symbols: its ruler and his god are
usually associated with the sun, the source of visibility. A visual
image of authority immobilizes the body, brings it to a respectful halt before a manifestation of loyalty or obedience. The revolutionary monotheism of the Bible develops a hatred of "idolatry," and an idol is essentially a visual image of something
authoritative or numinous in society or nature. For Biblical
monotheism there is nothing numinous in nature: all the divinities that have been discovered in nature are devils, and the

chosen people listen to the voice of its invisible God. The shift
from visual to aural metaphors, the stress on the hearing of the
word, is essential to a revolutionary attitude. The eye was satisfied in the Garden of Eden, and will be again at the end of
time, but throughout history we depend on the ear. In the Old
Testament there is never any difficulty about hearing God, but
in even the greatest visions, those of Isaiah and Ezekiel, what is
actually seen is much vaguer, and in the earlier books editorial
redactions cluster thickly around anything that might be interpreted as a direct vision of God. The emphasis on a received
canon of sacred writings, and the drawing of rigid boundary
lines against the closest heresies, such as the cult of high places
in the northern kingdom, are also aspects of a revolutionary
mentality, and similar features reappear in Marxism in our own
time.

The Hebrews seem to have been a rather unhandy people, not
distinguished for sculpture or building or even pottery, and the
contrast with Greek culture is instructive. In a polytheistic
religion one has to have statues or pictures to distinguish one
god from another, and Greek culture was focused on two intensely visual emblems: the nude in sculpture, and the theatre
in literature, the theatre being, as the etymology of the word
indicates, a primarily visual experience. We notice how often,
in the Christian tradition, movements of iconoclasm recur, associated with a dislike and distrust of religious painting, sculpture, and stained glass, as well as the theatre itself. Such movements are usually rationalized as a return to the primitive purity
of Christian doctrine, and iconoclasm in Judaic and Islamic
traditions is even more deeply entrenched.

The Biblical narrative runs from th
time, and the Old Testament presents
tory from the creation of the world t
by Nebuchadnezzar. After that, the c
tive disappears, but there are episod
tory, such as the books of Maccabee
the creation and the flood, which
agree were myths, and myths very si
flood stories over the world, excep
tegrated into a religious vision of ur
then move on to legend and folk tale
thousand Philistines with the jawb
making an iron axe head float, whi
patterns of story. The reasons for tel
counting for the name of the place
said to have occurred, are equally fa

The accounts of Abraham and of
best called historical reminiscence.
torical kernel, but it seems clear t
nothing of any Exodus, just as Ron
the life of Christ. Eventually we m
tual history, to which we can attac
archaeological evidence. But it is c
tory, which tends to be simplist
Ahab, for example, is portrayed as
cept for one episode from a differe
as an able ruler, so convincingly a
the Biblical writer is not delibe
sources, or distorting the ones he

In t
defined
remini
actual
exaspe
use, ar
we are
Bible
historie
seem te
cal acc
haps th
the Bo
except
of nam
thentic

Bein
things.
minimi
the poe
provide
it must
said it
respect
phy. B
Achille
out of
doubtle
does nc

Bible. The degree to which the Bible does record actual events can perhaps never be exactly ascertained. In our day a writer who has had a considerable vogue, especially among students, Emmanuel Velikowsky, has written books to show that two of the most unlikely events recorded in the Bible, the sun standing still during a battle of Joshua's and the shadow of the dial going backward during the illness of Hezekiah, did take place in the way that they are described. What is significant here is that the Bible itself does not appear to regard confirming evidence from outside itself as really strengthening its case.

History emerges from chronicle as soon as we have a writer who can see chronicles as material for some other kind of form, an organizing form which is not simply sequence but a *mythos* or narrative. The principle of narrative is the basis on which the material is selected and arranged. The story is familiar of how Gibbon sat musing among the ruins of the Capitol in Rome, and how the idea of writing about the decline and fall, first of the city itself, then of the Roman Empire, took possession of him. Ahead of him was still a vast body of sources, but he had the essential thing, the *mythos* of "decline and fall," and the *mythos* was the magic wand that he could use to make this monstrous brood of mental chaos obey his will.

The historical narrative in the Bible is not really a history but a *mythos* or narrative principle on which historical incidents are strung. We soon realize that we are being told the same story over and over again, and that this story is U-shaped. Israel starts in a condition of relative peace, independence, and prosperity, disobeys or forsakes its God, meets with disaster, plunges into humiliation, slavery, and exile, and then a God-appointed re-

deemer starts it on the way back to its original state. This
U-shaped *mythos* of fall into bondage and redemption to freedom
is not confined to the historical narrative: the entire Christian
Bible is enclosed by the story of Adam, who loses the tree and
water of life on the first page of Genesis and gets them back on
the last page of Revelation. We find the same pattern in the
story of Job, who loses and regains all he has, and in the parable
of the prodigal son—which incidentally is the only version in
which the protagonist himself determines the point of his return. It is a *mythos* closely related to that of comedy in literature, with the same pattern of descent into threatening or actual
complications reversed by some providential redemption. Directly opposed to it, and forming the background against it, is
the *mythos* of the recurring rise and fall of heathen empires. This
vision is tragic and ironic: the social unit, whatever it is, first
rises and then falls, forming an inverted-U shape like that of a
hero's role in a tragedy.

In a religious context there is usually a suggestion that there
is something in the rising of great powers opposed to the will of
God. This suggestion is not confined to Biblical writers. The
tremendous panorama in Herodotus, for example, comes to a
focus in the account of Xerxes' invasion of Greece, where all the
emphasis is on the invincibility of the invader. Many of the
Greeks went over to Persia at the outset; those who resisted
were hopelessly divided and mistrustful of each other; the great
hero Themistocles was a grafter; even the oracles were bribed
with Persian money. It was impossible that so demoralized a
rabble as the Greek resisters could have stopped the mighty Persian machine, but stop it they did. The moral for Herodotus,

apparently, is that the gods clearly don't like big empires. Something similar emerges from the Book of Daniel, written on the eve of the successful Maccabean resistance to the power of Syria. In Christian centuries the action of Providence, as a divine force intervening in human affairs, can be seen more clearly when you win: thus the storm that destroyed the Spanish Armada was providential to the English, but a natural event to the Spaniards. We notice that this sense of Providence is strongest in David-and-Goliath situations where, as in the battle of Agincourt, a big force is defeated by a much smaller one. In any case the rise and fall of Egypt, Assyria, Babylon, Persia, Greece, Syria, and Rome forms the historical background to the Bible, and is presented as a series of repetitions of what is spiritually the same event. In the Book of Revelation the approaching fall of the secular Roman power is identified with the fall of Babylon, and the author speaks of "that great city, which spiritually is called Sodom and Egypt."

Biblical scholars distinguish what they call *Weltgeschichte* and *Heilsgeschichte,* world history and spiritual history. It seems to me that the essential *mythos* of *Weltgeschichte* in the Bible is the inverted-U or negative cycle, the rise and fall of aggregates of human power, and that the essential *mythos* of *Heilsgeschichte* is the U-shaped positive cycle, the fall and rise again of a representative of humanity itself, Adam or Israel or Job, whose period of exile is ended by a power beyond humanity. The symbol of the end of the rise is Moses on top of a mountain seeing the Promised Land, or Elijah going up in a chariot of fire, or Job contemplating God's leviathan, or Jesus ascending into the sky. Nobody in history has ever seen the Promised Land: what we get in history is Joshua's conquest of Canaan, which starts the cycle turning once more. At the beginning of the Acts of the Apostles, Jesus ascends to heaven, but the Holy Spirit, the third person of the Trinity, comes down and begins the history of the Christian Church. It looks as though it were the power to go beyond history that provides the energy for a new historical cycle: in any case, the U-shaped pattern never turns into a closed circle, with the end exactly identical with the beginning.

Man's inability to learn anything "from" his own history has often been lamented, and there is a recurrent desire to use history as a moral parable. But nothing ever repeats itself in precisely the same conditions, hence trying to learn from history is a precarious enterprise. Besides, history usually has to be arranged a good deal before it will fit the parable form, and, in general, historical parables are to history much what bestiaries are to zoology. The same thing is true of the cultural histories based on value judgements, which imitate the U and the inverted-U patterns of Biblical history, but are pseudo-historical constructs. The historical view of Renaissance humanism, which was close to that of Gibbon's *mythos,* saw Classical and more particularly Roman culture as reaching the height of a Golden Age under Augustus, then declining through less expensive metals until we reach the Dark Ages, where Latin develops rhyme and accentual rhythm and similar horrors, until the Renaissance began to complete the U turn. Ruskin's *Stones of Venice* presents us with the opposite construct: here we have an inverted U, rising with the "servile art" of the pre-Gothic period to the height of Gothic itself in the thirteenth century, then declining through the "fall" (Ruskin's word) of the Renaissance to modern cific name and is about to enter history in a highly partisan role, taking the side of an oppressed people against their overlords. There even seems to be some evidence that the word "Hebrew" itself, back in Abraham's time, originally meant something more like "proletariat" than a conventional name for a people. Two features of a revolutionary mind are particularly important for us here. First, it is a dialectical and polarizing mind: whatever is not for it is against it, and it seeks to reduce or eliminate all middle ground, all liberal, eclectic, or "revisionist" attitudes. God consistently speaks of himself as "jealous," intolerant of any deviation in ritual or doctrine. Many gods are not different aspects of him: they are his enemies: like an earthly ruler, he can tolerate only subordinates. Second, a revolutionary mind is intensely concentrated on a reversal of the social order which is bound to occur in the future, a future which may be simply future time, or, as in apocalyptic literature, the end of time, but which is made, in the writer's expectations, as near and as imminent as he can get it.

Imperial monotheism reflects a strong and secure human order that feels able to come to terms with the order of nature. It expresses itself in visual symbols: its ruler and his god are usually associated with the sun, the source of visibility. A visual image of authority immobilizes the body, brings it to a respectful halt before a manifestation of loyalty or obedience. The revolutionary monotheism of the Bible develops a hatred of "idolatry," and an idol is essentially a visual image of something authoritative or numinous in society or nature. For Biblical monotheism there is nothing numinous in nature: all the divinities that have been discovered in nature are devils, and the chosen people listen to the voice of its invisible God. The shift from visual to aural metaphors, the stress on the hearing of the word, is essential to a revolutionary attitude. The eye was satisfied in the Garden of Eden, and will be again at the end of time, but throughout history we depend on the ear. In the Old Testament there is never any difficulty about hearing God, but in even the greatest visions, those of Isaiah and Ezekiel, what is actually seen is much vaguer, and in the earlier books editorial redactions cluster thickly around anything that might be interpreted as a direct vision of God. The emphasis on a received canon of sacred writings, and the drawing of rigid boundary lines against the closest heresies, such as the cult of high places in the northern kingdom, are also aspects of a revolutionary mentality, and similar features reappear in Marxism in our own time.

The Hebrews seem to have been a rather unhandy people, not distinguished for sculpture or building or even pottery, and the contrast with Greek culture is instructive. In a polytheistic religion one has to have statues or pictures to distinguish one god from another, and Greek culture was focused on two intensely visual emblems: the nude in sculpture, and the theatre in literature, the theatre being, as the etymology of the word indicates, a primarily visual experience. We notice how often, in the Christian tradition, movements of iconoclasm recur, associated with a dislike and distrust of religious painting, sculpture, and stained glass, as well as the theatre itself. Such movements are usually rationalized as a return to the primitive purity of Christian doctrine, and iconoclasm in Judaic and Islamic traditions is even more deeply entrenched.

The Biblical narrative runs from the beginning to the end of time, and the Old Testament presents a roughly continuous history from the creation of the world to the capture of Jerusalem by Nebuchadnezzar. After that, the continuous historical narrative disappears, but there are episodic indications of later history, such as the books of Maccabees. We start with stories of the creation and the flood, which most readers today would agree were myths, and myths very similar to other creation and flood stories over the world, except that they have been integrated into a religious vision of unique scope and power. We then move on to legend and folk tale, stories of Samson killing a thousand Philistines with the jawbone of an ass or of Elisha making an iron axe head float, which again belong to familiar patterns of story. The reasons for telling such stories, such as accounting for the name of the place where such an incident is said to have occurred, are equally familiar.

The accounts of Abraham and of the Exodus belong in an area best called historical reminiscence. They must contain some historical kernel, but it seems clear that Egyptian history knows nothing of any Exodus, just as Roman history knows nothing of the life of Christ. Eventually we move into what looks like actual history, to which we can attach some dates and supporting archaeological evidence. But it is didactic and manipulated history, which tends to be simplistic in its approach to facts. Ahab, for example, is portrayed as a kind of sinister clown, except for one episode from a different source which presents him as an able ruler, so convincingly as to make us wonder whether the Biblical writer is not deliberately preferring less reliable sources, or distorting the ones he has.

In this narrative there is no boundary line anywhere clearly defined that separates myth from legend, legend from historical reminiscence, reminiscence from didactic history, didactic from actual history. The Bible, considered as history, is a baffling and exasperating document which the historian has to learn how to use, and it creates more problems than it solves. The inference we are interested in at the moment is: if there is anything in the Bible which is historically accurate, it is not there because it is historically accurate, but for quite different reasons. The reasons seem to involve what we may call spiritual significance. Historical accuracy has no relation to spiritual significance, unless perhaps the relation is an inverse one. The spiritual significance of the Book of Job, which nobody has ever thought of as anything except an imaginative drama, is obviously greater than the lists of names in the Book of Chronicles, which may well contain authentic records.

Being aware of history and being historical are different things. A hundred years ago, critics of Homer were inclined to minimize the historical basis of the Trojan War and assume that the poet made it up out of his own head. Schliemann began to provide some archaeological evidence (of a very equivocal kind, it must be said) that there was a city more or less where Homer said it was, and since then scholars have acquired a considerable respect for Homer's sense of fact, in both history and geography. But no increasing respect for such matters will make Achilles' fight with the river-god or the hurling of Hephaistos out of heaven less mythical: those are as mythical as ever, and doubtless always will be. More simply, Homer's sense of history does not mean that he is writing history. Similarly with the

Bible. The degree to which the Bible does record actual events can perhaps never be exactly ascertained. In our day a writer who has had a considerable vogue, especially among students, Emmanuel Velikowsky, has written books to show that two of the most unlikely events recorded in the Bible, the sun standing still during a battle of Joshua's and the shadow of the dial going backward during the illness of Hezekiah, did take place in the way that they are described. What is significant here is that the Bible itself does not appear to regard confirming evidence from outside itself as really strengthening its case.

History emerges from chronicle as soon as we have a writer who can see chronicles as material for some other kind of form, an organizing form which is not simply sequence but a *mythos* or narrative. The principle of narrative is the basis on which the material is selected and arranged. The story is familiar of how Gibbon sat musing among the ruins of the Capitol in Rome, and how the idea of writing about the decline and fall, first of the city itself, then of the Roman Empire, took possession of him. Ahead of him was still a vast body of sources, but he had the essential thing, the *mythos* of "decline and fall," and the *mythos* was the magic wand that he could use to make this monstrous brood of mental chaos obey his will.

The historical narrative in the Bible is not really a history but a *mythos* or narrative principle on which historical incidents are strung. We soon realize that we are being told the same story over and over again, and that this story is U-shaped. Israel starts in a condition of relative peace, independence, and prosperity, disobeys or forsakes its God, meets with disaster, plunges into humiliation, slavery, and exile, and then a God-appointed re-

deemer starts it on the way back to its original state. This
U-shaped *mythos* of fall into bondage and redemption to freedom
is not confined to the historical narrative: the entire Christian
Bible is enclosed by the story of Adam, who loses the tree and
water of life on the first page of Genesis and gets them back on
the last page of Revelation. We find the same pattern in the
story of Job, who loses and regains all he has, and in the parable
of the prodigal son—which incidentally is the only version in
which the protagonist himself determines the point of his return. It is a *mythos* closely related to that of comedy in literature, with the same pattern of descent into threatening or actual
complications reversed by some providential redemption. Directly opposed to it, and forming the background against it, is
the *mythos* of the recurring rise and fall of heathen empires. This
vision is tragic and ironic: the social unit, whatever it is, first
rises and then falls, forming an inverted-U shape like that of a
hero's role in a tragedy.

In a religious context there is usually a suggestion that there
is something in the rising of great powers opposed to the will of
God. This suggestion is not confined to Biblical writers. The
tremendous panorama in Herodotus, for example, comes to a
focus in the account of Xerxes' invasion of Greece, where all the
emphasis is on the invincibility of the invader. Many of the
Greeks went over to Persia at the outset; those who resisted
were hopelessly divided and mistrustful of each other; the great
hero Themistocles was a grafter; even the oracles were bribed
with Persian money. It was impossible that so demoralized a
rabble as the Greek resisters could have stopped the mighty Persian machine, but stop it they did. The moral for Herodotus,

apparently, is that the gods clearly don't like big empires. Something similar emerges from the Book of Daniel, written on the eve of the successful Maccabean resistance to the power of Syria. In Christian centuries the action of Providence, as a divine force intervening in human affairs, can be seen more clearly when you win: thus the storm that destroyed the Spanish Armada was providential to the English, but a natural event to the Spaniards. We notice that this sense of Providence is strongest in David-and-Goliath situations where, as in the battle of Agincourt, a big force is defeated by a much smaller one. In any case the rise and fall of Egypt, Assyria, Babylon, Persia, Greece, Syria, and Rome forms the historical background to the Bible, and is presented as a series of repetitions of what is spiritually the same event. In the Book of Revelation the approaching fall of the secular Roman power is identified with the fall of Babylon, and the author speaks of "that great city, which spiritually is called Sodom and Egypt."

Biblical scholars distinguish what they call *Weltgeschichte* and *Heilsgeschichte,* world history and spiritual history. It seems to me that the essential *mythos* of *Weltgeschichte* in the Bible is the inverted-U or negative cycle, the rise and fall of aggregates of human power, and that the essential *mythos* of *Heilsgeschichte* is the U-shaped positive cycle, the fall and rise again of a representative of humanity itself, Adam or Israel or Job, whose period of exile is ended by a power beyond humanity. The symbol of the end of the rise is Moses on top of a mountain seeing the Promised Land, or Elijah going up in a chariot of fire, or Job contemplating God's leviathan, or Jesus ascending into the sky. Nobody in history has ever seen the Promised Land: what we get in history is Joshua's conquest of Canaan, which starts the cycle turning once more. At the beginning of the Acts of the Apostles, Jesus ascends to heaven, but the Holy Spirit, the third person of the Trinity, comes down and begins the history of the Christian Church. It looks as though it were the power to go beyond history that provides the energy for a new historical cycle: in any case, the U-shaped pattern never turns into a closed circle, with the end exactly identical with the beginning.

Man's inability to learn anything "from" his own history has often been lamented, and there is a recurrent desire to use history as a moral parable. But nothing ever repeats itself in precisely the same conditions, hence trying to learn from history is a precarious enterprise. Besides, history usually has to be arranged a good deal before it will fit the parable form, and, in general, historical parables are to history much what bestiaries are to zoology. The same thing is true of the cultural histories based on value judgements, which imitate the U and the inverted-U patterns of Biblical history, but are pseudo-historical constructs. The historical view of Renaissance humanism, which was close to that of Gibbon's *mythos,* saw Classical and more particularly Roman culture as reaching the height of a Golden Age under Augustus, then declining through less expensive metals until we reach the Dark Ages, where Latin develops rhyme and accentual rhythm and similar horrors, until the Renaissance began to complete the U turn. Ruskin's *Stones of Venice* presents us with the opposite construct: here we have an inverted U, rising with the "servile art" of the pre-Gothic period to the height of Gothic itself in the thirteenth century, then declining through the "fall" (Ruskin's word) of the Renaissance to modern times. If we compare these two views with one another, our final conclusion has to be, however much we may have incidentally learned from them, that neither of them has any real content. Like everything else founded on value judgements, sooner or later we have to throw them away and start again with genuine data.

History conceived as parable can be applied to the present only very indirectly and morally, by the individual, not by a programme of social or cultural action. This is the old *exemplum* theory of the usefulness of history, in which, say, the stories of Esther and Judith supply us with models of patriotic heroism, which we may admire but can apply to our own behavior only in the most oblique way. In such a moral and individual context Biblical history can be parable, with the parable's epilogue: "go thou and do likewise," or, more frequently, "go thou and avoid doing likewise." But, we are told by so many critics from Aristotle onward, this exemplary approach to history is more the concern of poetry than of history itself. The historical narrative of the Bible, which arranges everything with a view to bringing out its central *mythos* shape, along with the moral principles implied by that shape, is much closer to poetry than it is to actual history, and should be read as such. At this point the word *mythos* begins to turn into the word myth, and we have to face the possiblity that the entire Bible has to be read in the same way that most of us now read the story of Noah's ark.

The ordinary notion of myth and history is that history is what really happened; myth is what probably didn't happen, at least not in that form. The historian, we feel, tries to recapture the past in the present: if he is writing about Julius Caesar's assassination, he tries to show us what we might have seen if we had been present at the event. Truth, in this context, means truth of correspondence: a history, or structure of words is aligned with a body of human actions and is judged true if it is a satisfactory verbal replica of those actions. But truth of correspondence is not the concern of the literary critic: he deals entirely with verbal forms which are not primarily related to external facts or to propositions, and are never true in that context. To paraphrase Duke Theseus in Shakespeare, the poet, like the lover and the lawyer, is incapble of telling the truth by correspondence. So far as truth is involved in poetry, it is contained within the verbal form and provides no external criterion for it.

However acutely conscious I may be of my deficiencies as a Biblical scholar, I cannot be entirely unaware of the deficiencies of Biblical scholars as literary critics. Real literary criticism of the Bible, in the sense of a criticism that takes seriously its mythical and metaphorical aspect, has barely begun. Myth and metaphor are still often regarded as things to be apologized for, and scholars still speak hesitantly of "mythical elements" in Genesis or the Gospels, as though they were elements that could be, and therefore should be, removed. In Biblical terms, literary criticism is "higher" criticism, the criticism that is supposed to start after a certain amount of work has been done on establishing the text. But for all the to-do made about it a century ago, there has been no higher criticism of the Bible until very recently. Lower criticism, or genuine textual scholarship, has been followed by a still lower, or sub-basement, criticism, where the disintegrating of the text becomes an end in itself. Dozens of books tell us that the account of creation with which the Book of Genesis opens comes from the Priestly narrative, historically much the latest of the four major documents that make up the Pentateuch. If the scholar saying this were a genuine "higher" critic, his next sentence ought to say that this account of creation stands at the beginning of Genesis, not because it was written first, but because it belongs at the beginning of Genesis. The third sentence would land him in a full-scale critical analysis of the Book of Genesis, and eventually of the whole Bible, as it now stands. What one needs is a criticism that, instead of trying to cut away the myth as an accretion and retreat into some hypothetical embryonic stage of textual development, would tell us something about why the books of the Bible exist as they now do in their present form.

Such an obsession with disunity is a narrowly historical obsession, an inability to understand that there are forms of truth, meaning, and significance which are not dependent on correspondence with facts or other external criteria. The reason why the procedure is futile is that there is, quite simply, no end to it. If we start to "demythologize" the Gospels, for example, as some theologians urge us to do, trying to throw out everything that seems incredible, or suggested by something in the Old Testament or contemporary Jewish ritual or teaching, in quest of some historical core of events of which we can say "this at least must have happened," we shall find that we have thrown out so much of the Gospels that not one syllable of any of the four of them is left. No advance is possible until we reverse the procedure, accept the whole Bible as an imaginative unity of myth and metaphor, and see what comes out of that hypothesis.

What comes out of it is, among other things, the entire

structure of post-classical European literature, for which the
Bible provided a mythical and metaphorical framework. Another is the fact which, in the age of Heidegger and Wittgen-
stein, we are finally returning to: that poetic language is primary language, and that what words do with the greatest power
and accuracy is hang together, that is, form mythical and metaphorical entities. Poetic statements are not distorted or secondary forms of so-called "literal" statements: "literal" statements
are distorted and secondary forms of poetic ones. Words certainly have their descriptive uses, but these are of limited help if
we are trying to investigate the kind of world that the Bible
seems to lead us to: a world in which truth is a person or a personal God, and in which all men make up, not the aggregate
"mankind," but a single man. The Bible, taking it at its own
valuation, is far too important a book to contain any "truth," as
that word is generally understood.

At this point we may begin to suspect that myth is not simply unhistorical event, and metaphor not simply a non-concep-
tual form of thinking, but that they are anti-historical and anti-
conceptual, and are being used in the Bible for that reason.
How, we may ask, could a book regarded for so long, and by so
many, as a sacred book, a divine revelation, ever have been supposed to be speaking any other language? Surely a myth, or self-
contained verbal structure in which the recurring exile and return of Israel forms a counterpoint against the contrary movement of the rise and fall of heathen empires, is the only way of
giving any sense of *Heilsgeschichte,* or history as seen from
beyond history. Man is continually throwing up great intellectual anxiety structures, like spiritual geodesic domes, around his

culture and social institutions. If a book is believed to originate
from a source beyond the limitations of the human mind, and a
benevolent source at that, one would expect it to speak the language of breakthrough, a language that would smash these
structures beyond repair, and let some genuine air and light in.
But that, of course, is not how anxiety operates.

We have to move, therefore, from the historical and doctrinal
to the poetic and literary in getting a better understanding of
the Bible. It is possible to stop there with great profit: if we are
looking at the Bible without commitment, in the context, say,
of "comparative religion," this is in fact where we have to stop.
But the limitations of stopping here are equally obvious, so obvious that I have to make some comment on it even at the risk
of going beyond the concerns of the English Institute. It sounds
absurd to say that the Bible is a work of art or an epic poem like
the *Iliad* or the *Mahabharata,* although the statement is really
less absurd than it sounds. "Epic poem" is clearly the wrong
classification, but the sense of absurdity comes mainly from the
total critical ignorance of the literary and rhetorical issues connected with scriptures and sacred books. Still, there is unmis-
takably a sense in which the Bible transcends the poetic as well
as the historical. Even Blake, for all his devotion to both the
Bible and the arts, did not call the Bible a work of art: he called
it the "Great Code" of art.

For the historian, what is true is what is credible: the miraculous or the fabulous tend to get squeezed out of history even if
the historian believes them. What is credible corresponds to
what we encounter in ordinary experience. To adopt standards
of credibility is a serious thing to do, and one can understand

why the literary approach, which by-passes the issue of credibility altogether, should in some contexts come to be thought of as not very serious. The distinction between fact and fiction is essential to sanity; in reading a newspaper we want to know whether the stories in it are true or only made up, and if we have no means of knowing, the society we live in is, like the society in *1984,* deliberately trying to keep us mad. History tells us of real events that we can assimilate to our ordinary experience because they are more or less what we should have experienced at the time. Poetry tells us of events that are real, not in the sense of having happened just like that, but in the sense of being the kind of thing that is always happening. There is a third category: the actual event which is probably nothing like what we should have experienced if we had been "there." The assumption here is that in some events, at least, our ordinary experience does not tell us what is really happening.

In the last dozen years or so, with all the emphasis on separate realities, altered states of consciousness, and the like, we should be able at least to conceive the possibility of thinking in such terms. The Biblical prophets were usually ecstatics capable of going into trance states and speaking with what they called the voice of God. But it is clear that with, for example, Isaiah, this ecstatic power was not something separate from conscious intelligence, as it would be in a medium or the priestess of an oracle, but was simply an additional dimension of experience. Neither was it the same kind of thing as the creative imagination of a poet, even though it expressed itself in poetic language, as any language of such intensity would have to do. It was rather a description of experience as it appears to a higher state of consciousness. The word "higher" may beg a question, but the question certainly is begged in the Bible, or rather seized. Similarly in the Gospels, where it seems clear that the ordinary experience of those who were "there," including the disciples, took in very little of what the Gospel says was really going on at the time.

The danger of returning to square one still confronts us, for there is no going back to ordinary historical canons. A structure of myth and metaphor is what we have: it is all that we have, and it is no use trying to shake a residue of factual history out of it, even on a spiritual level. We may say, for example, that some Biblical stories seem to deal with really central issues, like the five versions of the Resurrection story, and that these may be the spiritual forms of real events. Others, like the stories of Samson, seem to be clearly folk tales, or at best allegories, while still others, like the story of Job, are explicitly poetical. But as long as we keep steadily looking at the whole Bible as a seamless web of myth and metaphor, this reductive solution becomes increasingly unsatisfying. If we want to go from the imaginative to the existential, we have to try to take a step forward from our literary understanding, in the opposite direction from the historical. Belief, as ordinarily understood, is a matter of credibility reinforced by credulity. But, as Tertullian suggested long ago, there may be such a thing as a belief which is the opposite of anything based on credibility.

The real step forward comes when we see that the entire Biblical vision, from Genesis to Revelation (or Chronicles in Judaism), may be spiritually present in every particular event, and may be in fact the genuine form of that event. But the only particular events that we can apply this principle to are the events of our own lives. Our credible historical lives form a part of *Weltgeschichte:* they rise and decline; they end in death, and whatever successes or triumphs they may include, there is always more frustration than fulfilment in them, no less than in the histories of Assyria or Rome. We can imagine another perspective on that life, a U-shaped perspective in which the real progression is the reverse of this, beginning in Eden or a Promised Land and ending like the story of the returned prodigal or the restored Job. Once this is seen as a part of *Heilsgeschichte,* conceived as the spiritual reality in contrast to the natural reality of what happens, we have started to go beyond imagination. This view of life is incredible, especially in its beginning and its end, and the proofs of its reality are not given: they are what it is up to us to supply.

The world of *Weltgeschichte* is a series of repetitions within a framework of compulsion and fatality: it is the world of the Viconian *ricorso,* and of Platonic *anamnesis,* or recollection, where we can know only by *re*-cognizing or seeing once again what we already know. In the world conveyed to us through the language of myth and metaphor, repetition is the power to make a new beginning, the power associated with humility in Eliot's "East Coker," because he thinks of humility as the opposite of the pride that continually builds the tower of Babel out of a confusion of tongues. The Biblical symbol of this new beginning is the rebuilt temple which marks the end of exile. This is the kind of repetition that regains time in Proust, that delivers us in *Finnegans Wake* from the returning history that Stephen Dedalus in *Ulysses* calls the nightmare from which he is trying to awake, that leads Dante in the *Purgatorio* upwards to his original identity in the Garden of Eden, and that enables Eliot finally to describe history itself as a pattern of timeless moments.

It is only the language of the imagination that can take us beyond imagination. Two inferences follow, for students of literature. First, the Bible demands a literary response from us, hence the study of literature has to expand a good deal beyond its usual limits. No book could have had the Bible's literary influence without itself possessing a literary form, however many other things it may also possess. There is also the question of the mythological framework which the Bible has provided for Western literature, already mentioned, and which is part of what Blake's phrase "Great Code of Art" means. Similar frameworks have been provided for other cultures by other sacred books: if one is attempting a serious study of Islamic literature, one has to begin with the Koran as a piece of literature. The second inference is that, as the mythical and metaphorical language spoken by literature is primary language, and the only means of reaching any spiritual reality beyond language, then, if such reality exists, works of literature themselves represent a practically untapped source of self-transforming power.

HAYDEN WHITE

✎⧳⧳✎

The Fictions of Factual Representation

In order to anticipate some of the objections with which historians often meet the argument that follows, I wish to grant at the outset that *historical events* differ from *fictional events* in the ways that it has been conventional to characterize their differences since Aristotle. Historians are concerned with events which can be assigned to specific time-space locations, events which are (or were) in principle observable or perceivable, whereas imaginative writers—poets, novelists, playwrights—are concerned with both these kinds of events and imagined, hypothetical, or invented ones. The nature of the kinds of events with which historians and imaginative writers are concerned is not the issue. What should interest us in the discussion of "the literature of fact" or, as I have chosen to call it, "the fictions of factual representation" is the extent to which the discourse of the historian and that of the writer of imaginative fictions overlap, resemble, or correspond with each other. Although historians and writers of fiction may be interested in different kinds of events, both the forms of their respective discourses and their aims in writing are often the same. In addition, in my view, the techniques or strategies that they use in the composition of their discourses can be shown to be substantially the same, however different they may appear on a purely surface, or dictional, level of their texts.

Readers of histories and novels can hardly fail to be struck by their similarities. There are many histories that could pass for novels, and many novels that could pass for histories, considered in purely formal (or, I should say, formalist) terms. Viewed simply as verbal artifacts histories and novels are indistinguishable from one another. We cannot easily distinguish between them on formal grounds unless we approach them with specific preconceptions about the kinds of truths that each is supposed to deal in. But the aim of the writer of a novel must be the same as that of the writer of a history. Both wish to provide a verbal image of "reality." The novelist may present his notion of this reality indirectly, that is to say, by figurative techniques, rather than directly, which is to say, by registering a series of propositions which are supposed to correspond point by point to some extra-textual domain of occurrence or happening, as the historian claims to do. But the image of reality which the novelist thus constructs is meant to correspond in its general outline to some domain of human experience which is no less "real" than that referred to by the historian. It is not, then, a matter of a conflict between two kinds of truth (which the Western prejudice for empiricism as the sole access to reality has foisted upon us), a conflict between the truth of correspondence, on the one side, and the truth of coherence, on the other. Every history must meet standards of coherence no less than those of correspondence if it is to pass as a plausible account of "the way things *really* were." For the empiricist prejudice is attended by a conviction that "reality" is not only perceivable but is also coherent in its structure. A mere list of confirmable singular existential statements does not add up to an account of reality if there is not some coherence, logical or aesthetic, connecting them one to another. So too every fiction must pass a test of correspondence (it must be "adequate" as an image of something beyond itself) if it is to lay claim to representing an insight into or illumination of the human experience of the world. Whether the events represented in a discourse are construed as atomic parts of a molar whole or as possible occurrences within a perceivable totality, the discourse taken in *its* totality as an image of some reality, bears a relationship of correspondence to that *of which* it is an image. It is in these twin senses that all written discourse is cognitive in its aims and mimetic in its means. And this is true even of the most ludic and seemingly expressivist discourse, of poetry no less than of prose, and even of those forms of poetry which seem to wish to illuminate only "writing" itself. In this respect, history is no less a form of fiction than the novel is a form of historical representation.

This characterization of historiography as a form of fiction making is not likely to be received sympathetically by either historians or literary critics who, if they agree on little else, conventionally agree that history and fiction deal with distinct orders of experience and therefore represent distinct, if not opposed, forms of discourse. For this reason it will be well to say a few words about how this notion of the *opposition* of history to fiction arose and why it has remained unchallenged in Western thought for so long.

Prior to the French Revolution, historiography was conventionally regarded as a literary art. More specifically, it was regarded as a branch of rhetoric and its "fictive" nature generally recognized. Although eighteenth-century theorists distinguished rather rigidly (and not always with adequate philosophical justification) between "fact" and "fancy," they did not on the whole view historiography as a representation of the facts unalloyed by elements of fancy. While granting the general desirability of historical accounts that dealt in real, rather than imagined events, theorists from Bayle to Voltaire and De Mably recognized the inevitability of a recourse to fictive techniques in the *representation* of real events in the historical discourse. The eighteenth century abounds in works which distinguish between the "study" of history on the one side and the "writing" of history on the other. The "writing" was a literary, specifically rhetorical exercise, and the product of this exercise was to be assessed as much on literary as on scientific principles.

Here the crucial opposition was between "truth" and "error," rather than between "fact" and "fancy," with it being understood that many kinds of truth, even in history, could only be presented to the reader by means of fictional techniques of representation. These techniques were conceived to consist of rhetorical devices, tropes, figures, and schemata of words and thoughts, which, as described by the classical and Renaissance rhetoricians, were identical with the techniques of poetry in general. "Truth" was not equated with "fact," but with a combination of fact and the conceptual matrix within which it was appropriately located in the discourse. The imagination no less than the reason had to be engaged in any adequate representation of the truth; and this meant that the techniques of fiction-making were as necessary to the composition of a historical discourse as erudition might be.

In the early nineteenth century, however, it became conventional, at least among historians, to identify truth with fact and to regard fiction as the opposite of truth, hence as a hindrance to the understanding of reality rather than as a way of apprehending it. History came to be set over against fiction, and especially the novel, as the representation of the "actual" to the representation of the "possible" or only "imaginable." And thus was born the dream of a historical discourse that would consist of nothing but factually accurate statements about a realm of events which were (or had been) observable in principle, the arrangement of which in the order of their original occurrence would permit them to figure forth their true meaning or significance. Typically, the nineteenth-century historian's aim was to expunge every hint of the fictive, or merely imaginable, from his discourse, to eschew the techniques of the poet and orator, and to forego what were regarded as the intuitive procedures of the maker of fictions in his apprehension of reality.

In order to understand this development in historical thinking, it must be recognized that historiography took shape as a distinct scholarly discipline in the West in the nineteenth century against a background of a profound hostility to all forms of myth. Both the political Right and the political Left blamed mythic thinking for the excesses and failures of the Revolution. False readings of history, misconceptions of the nature of the historical process, unrealistic expectations about the ways that historical societies could be transformed—all these had led to

the outbreak of the Revolution in the first place, the strange course that Revolutionary developments followed, and the effects of Revolutionary activities over the long run. It became imperative to rise above any impulse to interpret the historical record in the light of party prejudices, utopian expectations, or sentimental attachments to traditional institutions. In order to find one's way among the conflicting claims of the parties which took shape during and after the Revolution, it was necessary to locate some standpoint of social perception that was truly "objective," truly "realistic." If social processes and structures seemed "demonic" in their capacity to resist direction, to take turns unforeseen, and to overturn the highest plans, frustrating the most heartfelt desires, then the study of history had to be de-mythified. But in the thought of the age, de-mythification of any domain of inquiry tended to be equated with the de-fictionalization of that domain as well.

The distinction between myth and fiction which is a commonplace in the thought of our own century was hardly grasped at all by many of the foremost ideologues of the early nineteenth century. Thus it came about that history, the realistic science par excellence, was set over against fiction as the study of the real versus the study of the merely imaginable. Although Ranke had in mind that form of the novel which we have since come to call "Romantic" when he castigated it as mere fancy, he manifested a prejudice shared by many of his contemporaries when he defined history as the study of the real and the novel as the representation of the imaginary. Only a few theorists, among whom J. G. Droysen was the most prominent, saw that it was impossible to write history without having recourse to the techniques of the orator and the poet. Most of the "scientific" historians of the age did not see that for every identifiable kind of novel, historians produced an equivalent kind of historical discourse. Romantic historiography produced its genius in Michelet, Realistic historiography its paradigm in Ranke himself, Symbolist historiography produced Burckhardt (who had more in common with Flaubert and Baudelaire than with Ranke), and Modernist historiography its prototype in Spengler. It was no accident that the Realistic novel and Rankean historicism entered their respective crises at roughly the same time.

There were, in short, as many "styles" of historical representation as there are discernible literary styles in the nineteenth century. This was not perceived by the historians of the nineteenth century because they were captives of the illusion that one could write history without employing any fictional techniques whatsoever. They continued to honor the conception of the opposition of history to fiction throughout the entire period, even while producing forms of historical discourse so different from one another that their grounding in aesthetic preconceptions of the nature of the historical process alone could explain those differences. Historians continued to believe that different interpretations of the same set of events were functions of ideological distortions or of inadequate factual data. They continued to believe that if one only eschewed ideology and remained true to the facts, history would produce a knowledge as certain as anything offered by the physical sciences and as objective as a mathematical exercise.

Most nineteenth-century historians did not realize that, when it is a matter of trying to deal with past facts, the crucial consideration for him who would represent them faithfully are the notions he brings to his representation of the ways parts relate to the whole which they comprise. They did not realize that the facts do not speak for themselves, but that the historian speaks for them, speaks on their behalf, and fashions the fragments of the past into a whole whose integrity is—in its *re*presentation—a purely discursive one. Novelists might be dealing only with imaginary events whereas historians are dealing with real ones, but the process of fusing events, whether imaginary or real, into a comprehensible totality capable of serving as the *object* of a representation, is a poetic process. Here the historian must utilize precisely the same tropological strategies, the same modalities of representing relationships in words, that the poet or novelist uses. In the unprocessed historical record and in the chronicle of events which the historian extracts from the record, the facts exist only as a congeries of contiguously related fragments. These fragments have to be put together to make a whole of a particular, not a general, kind. And they are put together in the same ways that novelists use to put together figments of their imaginations to display an ordered world, a cosmos, where only disorder or chaos might appear.

So much for manifestos. On what grounds can such a reactionary position be justified? On what grounds can the assertion that historical discourse shares more than it divides with novelistic discourse be sustained? The first ground is to be found in recent developments in literary theory—especially in the insistence by modern Structuralist and text critics on the necessity of dissolving the distinction between prose and poetry in order to identify their shared attributes as forms of linguistic behavior that are as much constitutive of their objects of representation as they are reflective of external reality, on the one side, and projective of internal emotional states, on the other. It appears that Stalin was right when he opined that language belonged neither to the Superstructure nor the Base of cultural praxis, but was, in some unspecified way, *prior to both.* We don't know the origin of language and never shall, but it is certain today that language is more adequately characterized as being neither a free creation of human consciousness nor merely a product of environmental forces acting on the psyche, but rather the *instrument of mediation* between consciousness and the world that consciousness inhabits.

This will not be news to literary theorists, but it has not yet reached the historians buried in the archives hoping, by what they call a "sifting of the facts" or "the manipulation of the data," to *find* the form of the reality that will serve as the object of representation in the account that they will write when "all the facts are known" and they have finally "got the story straight."

So, too, contemporary critical theory permits us to believe more confidently than ever before that "poetizing" is not an activity that hovers over, transcends, or otherwise remains alienated from life or reality, but represents a mode of praxis which serves as the immediate base of all cultural activity (this an insight of Vico, Hegel, and Nietzsche, no less than of Freud and Lévi-Strauss), even of science itself. We are no longer compelled, therefore, to believe—as historians in the post-Romantic period had to believe—that fiction is the antithesis of fact (in the way that superstition or magic is the antithesis of

science) or that we can relate facts to one another without the
aid of some enabling and generically fictional matrix. This too
would be news to many historians were they not so fetishis-
tically enamored of the notion of "facts" and so congenitally hos-
tile to "theory" in any form that the presence in a historical
work of a formal theory used to explicate the relationship between facts and concepts is enough to earn them the charge of
having defected to the despised "sociology" or of having lapsed
into the nefarious "philosophy of history."

Every discipline, I suppose, is, as Nietzsche saw most clearly,
constituted by what it *forbids* its practitioners to do. Every discipline is made up of a set of restrictions on thought and imagination, and none is more hedged about with taboos than professional historiography—so much so that the so-called "historical
method" consists of little more than the injunction to "get the
story straight" (without any notion of what the relation of
"story" to "fact" might be) and to avoid both conceptual over-
determination and imaginative excess (i.e., "enthusiasm") at
any price.

Yet the price paid is a considerable one. It has resulted in the
repression of the *conceptual apparatus* (without which atomic facts
cannot be aggregated into complex macro-structures and constituted as objects of discursive representation in a historical narrative) and the remission of the *poetic moment* in historical writing
to the interior of the discourse (where it functions as an unacknowledged—and therefore uncriticizable—*content* of the historical narrative).

Those historians who draw a firm line between history and
philosophy of history fail to recognize that every historical dis-

course contains within it a full blown—if only implicit—philosophy of history. And this is as true of what is conventionally called "narrative" (or diachronic) historiography as it is of "conceptual" (or synchronic) historical representation. The principal difference between history and philosophy of history is that the latter brings the conceptual apparatus by which the facts are ordered in the discourse to the surface of the text, while "history proper" (as it is called) buries it in the interior of the narrative, where it serves as a hidden or implicit shaping device, in precisely the same way that Professor Frye conceives his *archetypes* to do in narrative fictions. History does not therefore stand over against myth as its cognitive antithesis, but represents merely another, and more extreme form of that "displacement" which Professor Frye has analyzed in his *Anatomy*. Every history has its myth; and if there are different fictional modes based on different identifiable mythical archetypes, so too there are different historiographical modes—different ways of hypotactically ordering the "facts" contained in the chronicle of events occurring in a specific time-space location, such that events in the same set are capable of functioning differently in order to figure forth different *meanings*, moral, cognitive, or aesthetic, within different fictional matrices.

In fact, I would argue that these mythic modes are more easily identifiable in historiographical than they are in "literary" texts. For historians usually work with much less *linguistic* (and therefore less *poetic*) self-consciousness than writers of fiction do. They tend to treat language as a transparent vehicle of representation that brings no cognitive baggage of its own into the discourse. Great works of fiction will usually—if Roman Jakobson is right—not only be *about* their putative subject-matter, but also *about* language itself and the problematical relation between language, consciousness, and reality—including the writer's own language. Most historians' concern with language extends only to the effort to speak plainly, to avoid florid figures of speech, to assure that the persona of the author appears nowhere identifiable in the text, and to make clear what technical terms mean, when they dare to use any.

This is not, of course, the case with the great philosophers of history—from Augustine, Machiavelli, and Vico to Hegel, Marx, Nietzsche, Croce, and Spengler. The problematical status of language (including their own linguistic protocols) constitutes a crucial element in their own *apparatus criticus*. And it is not the case with the great classic writers of historiography—from Thucydides and Tacitus to Michelet, Carlyle, Ranke, Droysen, Tocqueville, and Burckhardt. These historians at least had a rhetorical self-consciousness that permitted them to recognize that any set of facts was variously, and equally legitimately, describable, that there is no such thing as a single correct original description of anything, on the basis of which an interpretation of that thing can *subsequently* be brought to bear. They recognized, in short, that all original descriptions of any field of phenomena are *already* interpretations of its structure, and that the linguistic mode in which the original description (or taxonomy) of the field is cast will implicitly rule out certain modes of representation and modes of explanation regarding the field's structure and tacitly sanction others. In other words, the favored mode of original description of a field of historical phenomena (and this includes the field of literary texts) already contains implicitly within it a limited range of modes of emplotment and modes of argument by which to disclose the meaning of the field in a discursive prose representation. If, that is, the description is anything more than a random registering of impressions. The plot-structure of a historical narrative (*how* things turned out as they did) and the formal argument or explanation of *why* "things happened or turned out as they did" are *pre*figured by the original description (of the "facts" to be explained) in a given dominant modality of language use: metaphor, metonymy, synecdoche, or irony.

Now, I want to make clear that I am myself using these terms as metaphors for the different ways we construe fields or sets of phenomena in order to "work them up" into *possible objects of narrative representation* and *discursive analysis*. Anyone who originally encodes the world in the mode of metaphor, will be inclined to decode it—that is, narratively "explicate" and discursively analyze it—as a congeries of individualities. To those for whom there is no real resemblance in the world, decodation must take the form of a disclosure, either of the simple *contiguity* of things (the mode of metonymy) or of the *contrast* that lies hidden within every apparent resemblance or unity (the mode of irony). In the first case, the narrative representation of the field, construed as a diachronic process, will favor as a privileged mode of emplotment the archetype of Romance and a mode of explanation that identifies knowledge with the appreciation and delineation of the particularity and individuality of things. In the second case, an original description of the field in the mode of metonymy will favor a tragic plot-structure as a privileged mode of emplotment and mechanistic causal connection as the

favored mode of explanation, to account for changes topographi-
cally outlined in the emplotment. So too an ironic original
description of the field will generate a tendency to favor emplotment in the mode of satire and pragmatic or contextual explanation of the structures thus illuminated. Finally, to round out
the list, fields originally described in the synecdochic mode will
tend to generate comic emplotments and organicist explanations
of why these fields change as they do.[1]

Note, for example, that both those great narrative hulks
produced by such classic historians as Michelet, Tocqueville,
Burckhardt, and Ranke, on the one side, and the elegant syn-
opses produced by philosophers of history such as Herder, Marx,
Nietzsche, and Hegel, on the other, become more easily relat-
able, one to the other, if we see them as both victims and
exploiters of the linguistic mode in which they originally describe a field of historical events *before* they apply their characteristic modalities of narrative representation and explanation, that
is, their "interpretations" of the field's "meaning." In addition,
each of the linguistic modes, modes of emplotment, and modes
of explanation has affinities with a specific ideological position:
anarchist, radical, liberal, and conservative respectively. The
issue of ideology points to the fact that there is no value-neutral
mode of emplotment, explanation, or even description of any
field of events, whether imaginary or real, and suggests that the
very use of language itself implies or entails a specific posture

[1] I have tried to exemplify at length each of these webs of relationships in
given historians in my book *Metahistory: The Historical Imagination in Nineteenth-Century Europe* (Baltimore & London: The Johns Hopkins Univ. Press,
1973).

before the world which is ethical, ideological, or more generally political: not only all interpretation, but also all language is politically contaminated.

Now, in my view, any historian who simply described a set of facts in, let us say, metonymic terms and then went on to emplot its processes in the mode of tragedy and proceeded to explain those processes mechanistically, and finally drew explicit ideological implications from it—as most vulgar Marxists and materialistic determinists do—would not only not be very interesting but could legitimately be labelled a *doctrinaire* thinker who had "bent the facts" to fit a preconceived theory. The peculiar dialectic of historical discourse—and of other forms of discursive prose as well, perhaps even the novel—comes from the effort of the author to mediate between alternative modes of emplotment and explanation, which means, finally, *mediating between alternative modes of language use* or *tropological* strategies for originally describing a given field of phenomena and constituting it as a possible object of representation.

It is this sensitivity to alternative linguistic protocols, cast in the modes of metaphor, metonymy, synecdoche, and irony, that distinguishes the great historians and philosophers of history from their less interesting counterparts among the technicians of these two crafts. This is what makes Tocqueville so much more interesting (and a source of so many different later thinkers) than either his contemporary, the doctrinaire Guizot, or most of his modern liberal or conservative followers, whose knowledge is greater than his and whose retrospective vision is more extensive but whose dialectical capacity is so much more weakly developed. Tocqueville writes about the French Revolution, but he writes even more meaningfully about the difficulty of ever attaining to a definitive *objective characterization* of the complex web of facts that comprise the Revolution as a graspable totality or structured whole. The contradiction, the *aporia,* at the heart of Tocqueville's discourse is born of his awareness that alternative, mutually exclusive, original descriptions of what the Revolution *is* are possible. He recognizes that *both* metonymical and synecdochic linguistic protocols can be used, equally legitimately, to describe the field of facts that comprise the "Revolution" and to constitute it as a *possible object* of *historical discourse.* He moves feverishly between the two modes of original description, testing both, trying to assign them to different mental sets or cultural types (what he means by a "democratic" consciousness is a metonymic transcription of phenomena; "aristocratic" consciousness is synecdochic). He himself is satisfied with neither mode, although he recognizes that each gives access to a specific aspect of reality and represents a possible way of apprehending it. His aim, ultimately, is to contrive a language capable of mediating between the two modes of consciousness which these linguistic modes represent. This aim of mediation, in turn, drives him progressively toward the ironic recognition that any given linguistic protocol will obscure as much as it reveals about the reality it seeks to capture in an order of words. This *aporia* or sense of contradiction residing at the heart of language itself is present in *all* of the classic historians. It is this linguistic self-consciousness which distinguishes them from their mundane counterparts and followers, who think that language can serve as a perfectly transparent medium of representation and who think that if one can only find the right language for describing events, the meaning of the events will *display itself* to consciousness.

This movement between alternative linguistic modes conceived as alternative descriptive protocols is, I would argue, a distinguishing feature of all of the great classics of the "literature of fact." Consider, for example, Darwin's *Origin of Species,*[2] a work which must rank as a classic in any list of the great monuments of this kind of literature. This work which, more than any other, desires to remain within the ambit of plain fact, is just as much about the problem of classification as it is about its ostensible subject matter, the data of natural history. This means that it deals with two problems: how are events to be described as possible elements of an argument; and what kind of argument do they add up to once they are so described?

Darwin claims to be concerned with a single, crucial question: "Why are not all organic things linked together in inextricable chaos?" (p. 453). But he wishes to answer this question in particular terms. He does not wish to suggest, as many of his contemporaries held, that all systems of classification are arbitrary, that is, mere products of the minds of the classifiers; he insists that there is a *real* order in nature. On the other hand, he does not wish to regard this order as a product of some spiritual or teleological power. The order which he seeks in the data, then, must be manifest in the facts themselves but not manifested in such a way as to display the operations of any transcendental power. In order to establish this notion of nature's plan,

---

[2] References in the text to Darwin's *Origin of Species* are to the Dolphin Edition (New York: Doubleday, n.d.).

he purports, first, simply to entertain "objectively" all of the "facts" of natural history provided by field naturalists, domestic breeders, and students of the geological record—in much the same way that the historian entertains the data provided by the archives. But this entertainment of the record is no simple reception of the facts; it is an entertainment of the facts with a view toward the discrediting of all previous taxonomic systems in which they have previously been encoded.

Like Kant before him, Darwin insists that the source of all error is semblance. Analogy, he says again and again, is always a "deceitful guide" (see pp. 61, 66, 473). As against analogy, or as I would say merely metaphorical characterizations of the facts, Darwin wishes to make a case for the existence of real "affinities" genealogically construed. The establishment of these affinities will permit him to postulate the linkage of all living things to all others by the "laws" or "principles" of genealogical descent, variation, and natural selection. These laws and principles are the formal elements in his mechanistic explanation of why creatures are arranged in families in a time series. But this explanation could not be offered as long as the data remained encoded in the linguistic modes of either metaphor or synecdoche, the modes of qualitative connection. As long as creatures are classified in terms of either semblance or essential unity, the realm of organic things must remain either a chaos of arbitrarily affirmed connectedness or a hierarchy of higher and lower forms. Science as Darwin understood it, however, cannot deal in the categories of the "higher" and "lower" any more than it can deal in the categories of the "normal" and "monstrous." Everything must be entertained as what it manifestly *seems to be.* Nothing can be regarded as "surprising," any more than anything can be regarded as "miraculous."

There are many kinds of facts invoked in *The Origin of Species:* Darwin speaks of "astonishing" facts (p. 301), "remarkable" facts (p. 384), "leading" facts (pp. 444, 447), "unimportant" facts (p 58), "well-established" facts, even "strange" facts (p. 105); but there are no "surprising" facts. Everything, for Darwin no less than for Nietzsche, is just what it appears to be—but what things appear to be are data inscribed under the aspect of *mere contiguity in space* (all the facts gathered by naturalists all over the world) *and time* (the records of domestic breeders and the geological record). As the elements of a problem (or rather, of a puzzle, for Darwin is confident that there is a solution to his problem), the facts of natural history are conceived to exist in that mode of relationship which is presupposed in the operation of the linguistic trope of metonymy, which is the favored trope of all *modern* scientific discourse (this is one of the crucial distinctions between modern and pre-modern sciences). The substitution of the name of a part of a thing for the name of the whole is pre-linguistically sanctioned by the importance which the scientific consciousness grants to mere contiguity. Considerations of *semblance* are tacitly retired in the employment of this trope, and so are considerations of *difference* and *contrast.* This is what gives to metonymic consciousness what Kenneth Burke calls its "reductive" aspect. Things exist in contiguous relationships that are only spatially and temporally definable. This metonymizing of the world, this preliminary encoding of the facts in terms of merely contiguous relationships, is necessary to the removal of metaphor and teleology from phenomena

which every *modern* science seeks to effect. And Darwin spends
the greater part of his book on the justification of this encodation, or original description, of reality, in order to discharge the
errors and confusion which a *merely* metaphorical profile of it has
produced.

But this is only a preliminary operation. Darwin then proceeds to restructure the facts—but *only along one axis* of the
time-space grid on which he has originally deployed them. Instead of stressing the mere contiguity of the phenomena, he
shifts gears, or rather tropological modes, and begins to concentrate on differences—but two kinds of differences: *variations
within species,* on the one side, and *contrasts between the species,* on
the other. "Systematists," he writes, ". . . have only to decide
. . . whether any form be sufficiently *constant* and *distinct* from
other forms, to be capable of definition; and if definable,
whether the differences be sufficiently important to deserve a
specific name." But the distinction between a species and a variety is only a matter of degree.

> Hereafter we shall be compelled to acknowledge that the only
> distinction between species and well-marked varieties is, that
> the latter are known, or believed, to be connected at the
> present day by intermediate gradation, whereas *species* were
> formerly thus connected. Hence, without rejecting the con-
> sideration of the *present existence* of intermediate gradations be-
> tween any two forms, we shall be led to weigh more carefully
> and to *value higher* the *actual amount of difference between them.*
> It is quite possible that forms now generally acknowledged to
> be merely varieties *may hereafter* be thought worthy of *specific*

names; and in this case *scientific and common language will come into accordance.* In short, we shall have to treat species in the same manner as those naturalists treat genera, who admit that genera are merely artificial combinations made for convenience. This may not be a cheering prospect; but we shall at least be free from the vain search for the undiscovered and undiscoverable *essence* of the term species. (pp. 474–75; italics added)

And yet Darwin has smuggled in his own conception of the "essence" of the term species. And he has done it by falling back on the geological record which, following Lyell, he calls "a history of the world imperfectly kept, . . . written in a changing dialect" and of which "we possess the last volume alone" (p. 331). Using this record, he postulates the descent of all species and varieties from some four or five prototypes governed by what he calls the "rule" of "gradual transition" (pp. 180 ff.) or "the great principle of gradation" (p. 251). *Difference* has been dissolved in the *mystery of transition,* such that *continuity-in-variation* is seen as the "rule" and radical discontinuity or variation as an "anomaly" (p. 33). But this "mystery" of transition (see his highly tentative, confused, and truncated discussion of the possible "modes of transition"—pp. 179–82, 310) is nothing but the facts laid out on a time line, rather than spatially disposed, and treated as a "series" which is permitted to *"impress . . . the mind* with the *idea of an actual passage"* (p. 66). All organic beings are then (gratuitously on the basis of both the facts and the theories available to Darwin) treated (metaphorically on the literal level of the text but synecdochically on the allegorical

level) as belonging to families linked by genealogical descent
(through the operation of variation and natural selection) from
the postulated four or five prototypes. It is only his distaste for
"analogy," he tells us, that keeps him from going "one step further, namely, to the belief that all plants and animals are descended from some one prototype" (p. 473). But he has approached as close to a doctrine of organic unity as his respect for
the "facts," in their original encodation in the mode of contiguity, will permit him to go. He has *transformed* "the facts"
from a structure of merely contiguously related particulars into a
sublimated synecdoche. And this in order to put a new and
more comforting (as well as, in his view, a more interesting and
comprehensible) vision of nature in place of that of his vitalistic
opponents.

The image which he finally offers—of an unbroken succession
of generations—may have had a disquieting effect on his readers, inasmuch as it dissolved the distinction between both the
"higher" and "lower" in nature (and by implication, therefore,
in society) and the "normal" and the "monstrous" in life (and
therefore in culture). But in Darwin's view, the new image of
organic nature as an essential continuity of beings gave assur-
ance that no "cataclysm" had ever "desolated the world" and
permitted him to look forward to a "secure future and progress
toward perfection" (p. 477). For "cataclysm" we can of course
read "revolution" and for "secure future," "social status quo."
But all of this is presented, not as image, but as plain fact.
Darwin is ironic only with respect to those systems of classification that would ground "reality" in fictions of which he does
not approve. Darwin distinguishes between tropological codes

that are "responsible" to the data and those that are not. But the criterion of responsibility to the data is not extrinsic to the operation by which the "facts" are ordered in his initial description of them; this criterion is intrinsic to that operation.

As thus envisaged, even the *Origin of Species,* that *summa* of "the literature of fact" of the nineteenth century, must be read as a kind of allegory—a history of nature meant to be understood literally but appealing ultimately to an image of coherency and orderliness which it constructs by linguistic "turns" alone. And if this is true of the *Origin,* how much more true must it be of any history of human societies? In point of fact, historians have no agreed upon terminological system for the description of the events which they wish to treat as facts and embed in their discourses as self-revealing data. Most historiographical disputes—among scholars of roughly equal erudition and intelligence—turn precisely on the matter of which among several linguistic protocols is to be used to *describe* the events under contention, not what explanatory system is to be applied to the events in order to reveal their meaning. Historians remain under the same illusion that had seized Darwin, the illusion that a value-neutral description of the facts, prior to their interpretation or analysis, was possible. It was not the doctrine of natural selection advanced by Darwin that commended him to other students of natural history as the Copernicus of natural history. That doctrine had been known and elaborated long before Darwin advanced it in the *Origin.* What had been required was a redescription of the facts to be explained in a language which would sanction the application to them of the doctrine as the most adequate way of explaining them.

And so too for historians seeking to "explain" the "facts" of the French Revolution, the decline and fall of the Roman Empire, the effects of slavery on American society, or the meaning of the Russian Revolution. What is at issue here is not: What are the facts? but rather: How are the facts to be described in order to sanction one mode of explaining them rather than another? Some historians will insist that history cannot become a science until it finds the technical terminology adequate to the correct characterization of its objects of study, in the way that physics did in the calculus and chemistry did in the periodic tables. Such is the recommendation of Marxists, Positivists, Cliometricians, and so on. Others will continue to insist that the integrity of historiography depends on its use of ordinary language, its avoidance of jargon. These latter suppose that ordinary language is a safeguard against ideological deformations of the "facts." What they fail to recognize is that ordinary language itself has its own forms of terminological determinism, represented by the figures of speech without which discourse itself is impossible.

VICTOR TURNER

❦

African Ritual and Western Literature: Is a Comparative Symbology Possible?

I have *assisted at* many performances of African ritual and *read* many works of European literature. The former's essence is kinesthetic, the latter's esthetic. You are moved literally by ritual, figuratively by literature. Action and intersubjectivity dominate ritual, reflection and subjectivity dominate reading. Both abound in symbols, but can ritual and literary symbols be meaningfully compared? The problem is placed in sharper focus by comparing genres drawn not from a single culture but from culture areas divergent to the point of apparent discrepancy. Only very remotely may central African ritual be genetically connected to European literature, and then perhaps typologically rather than historically, in the sense that in many cultures (those of Japan, China, India, ancient Hellas, and so on) ritual seems to have preceded drama as a major cultural form. Literature is composed by sedentary writers for sedentary readers. The writers may have in their time been involved in action, including ritual and dramatic action, but their works do not ensue from action, but rather from reflection upon it. (Melville did not write *Moby Dick* in a whaler's crow's-nest.) Readers relate authorial reflections to memories of their own actions. Individual reflection makes accessible to other individual minds a complicated written or printed message. Subjectivity encounters subjectivity through an objective medium of communication, the manuscript or book. The process is one-way; the writer beams out his message in the hope but not the certainty that it will be picked up by readers, but unless a reader is also a critic the writer will seldom get feedback from the subjectivities he tries to inseminate with his subjectivity. As Kierkegaard has said, it's like shouting a message to someone rushing past in the night.

In the rituals of preliterate peoples the situation is quite different. Here there is no question of a single author and a single reader, or, more generally, of a single transmitter and a single receiver. The form and content of a ritual, on the occasion of its most recent performance, derive, on the one hand, from recollections of previous performances in the heads of those publicly declared to be its masters of ceremonies, and, on the other, from the flair of those immediately engaged in it, those who appropriately relate traditional components to current social circumstances. Here, inheritance and innovation are both social; in a sense, *everyone* is both author and authored, maker and made. The liturgical armature is the product of past social action; the way that it is bent and stretched to fit the purposes of the moment is also socially determined. At all points there is reciprocity, interaction, communication, open or tacit.

Again, while sight and imagination dominate literature both for author and reader, neither direct nor indirect visualization exhaust the sensory codings of ritual. Hearing, touch, taste, smell, bodily movement are all drawn on to provide repertoires of formal elements, which are then orchestrated into intricately combined patterns of ritualized action. There is little that is "sedentary" about African ritual unless it is the role of a novice in an initiation rite or a patient in a therapeutic rite who must maintain a posture of still humility. But this passivity is itself dramatic; it is an attribute of a contrapuntal role which forms part of a system of roles, many of which are extremely active. Moreover, in other episodes the novice or patient may engage in vivid action, notable in the concluding, or "reaggregation," phase of a ritual.

This description of African ritual hardly resembles what we have until recently been accustomed to think of as religious liturgy or "church services" in the West. Perhaps this is because our rituals are deeply literate. They assume the authoritative transmission of words and gestures based on written rubrics and are often read from a written script to mainly passive receivers (who may, to be sure, at times, be allowed limited gestural responses but who are not encouraged to perform these in their own idiosyncratic ritual style as nearly everywhere occurs in the African case).

In any event I am not comparing African with Western liturgy, or Africal folk tales and epics with Western literary genres, I am deliberately making things harder for myself by symbologically comparing a sacred African genre of action, ritual, with Western literary modes. What highest common factors can we find? How may analysis of the former help us better to elucidate the latter and vice versa?

I

First, a few words on therapeutic (or healing) rituals and communities among the Ndembu of northwestern Zambia, a matrilineal people, about 7,000 in number, in whose company I did two-and-a-half-years field work. Like many other African peoples Ndembu use the same term for the malady or affliction and the procedures for curing or removing it. There are several kinds of cults of affliction, performed for individuals said by Ndembu to have been "caught" (or in some cases "bitten" or "smitten") by the shades of deceased relatives whom they have forgotten to honor with regular small gifts of crops and beer, or whom they have offended by omitting to mention by name when prayers are made at the village shrine trees planted in their memory. Very frequently people are allegedly "caught" for quarrelling with kin or village neighbors, or as representatives of village kin groups torn by quarrels. The ancestral shades act as a kind of collective conscience or "superego," punishing the social body by afflicting one or more of its constituent parts, which we would term "individuals." The Leibnitzian notion of a closed 'self' would not be recognized by the Ndembu. Selves are 'open' to one another, for good or ill. It is as though each self were festooned with prepositional cords and plugs (*with, among, to, for,* even *against*) and thus as though no individual could exist alone—only when plugged into his group or network.

Being "caught" by an ancestral shade means several things. Both sexes may be smitten by illness, men by bad luck at hunting, and women with reproductive disorders of certain specified types. Ndembu distinguish between the shade or spirit which afflicts and its mode of affliction. The shade is a known and named deceased relative of the afflicted person or patient, often one fairly recently dead. The *patient* is at the same time a *candidate* for admission into the curative cult community; the *doctor* is an *adept* in that cult. The *mode of affliction* refers to certain characteristics of the shade which are correlated with distinctive features of the patient's misfortune or illness. Mode of affliction and curative ritual have the same name, as I mentioned earlier. The therapeutic ritual is carried out by a number of doctor adepts, both male and female, who have themselves either been patients or else (as in the case of the male adepts in women's rituals) have been closely associated by kinship and affinity with afflicted patient candidates in previous performances of that type of ritual. Such adepts form a flexible *ad hoc* cult association whose members are mobilized to cure someone afflicted as they had once been. It is a community of suffering and "having suffered" people. Adepts each perform different tasks, but they *flow* into their roles rather than are assigned them in a hierarchical way.

Chihamba is the most complex and important of all the cults of affliction. Not only an ancestral shade but also a "territorial" or "tribal" spirit or demigod, whose secret cult name is *Kavula,* an archaic term for "lightning," are considered to be agencies of affliction. And this pair can bestow "all the ills that flesh is heir to" including bad luck at hunting upon those they have chosen for cult membership. *Kavula* is male, the afflicting shade is female. The principal candidates are women, but the leading adepts are men. *Kavula* transcends the localized, particularistic divisions into villages and chiefdoms; he is the whole land and all its changes of seasons. The ancestress betokens the village microcosm and the web of kinship linking different villages. Two domains and two logics here interlace. There is not monologic but dialogic form.

When the people of my village, Mukanza, decided to sponsor

a big *Chihamba* performance, they were perhaps driven to it by their internal state of dissension. Three of its factions were constantly contending for the headmanship, for the present headman was old and infirm; there were other sources of conflict, too. But like neurosis, affliction has "secondary gains." *Chihamba* was consciously manipulated to restore friendship not only within the village, but also with other villages. One village was indeed a split-off segment of Mukanza (founded by a group that had left the parent body after quarrels and witchcraft accusations). Others were linked to it by kinship, and divided from it by envy and conflicting material interests of various sorts. Here we have a microcosm of international diplomacy, with *Chihamba* as a sort of United Nations Building or Olympic Games. Anyway, practically everyone in any way connected with Mukanza village came along to participate as adepts or candidates in the secret or public phases of their ritual.[1]

This symbolic action can best be understood in relation to human social experiences of love and friendship, hatred and rivalry, social constraints and individual identity, determinacy and indeterminacy, continuity and discontinuity, which we too have felt and which enable us, with a little guidance as to natural, social, and cultural environmental conditions, to penetrate sympathetically the messages embodied in the ritual symbols.

By the time I took part in *Chihamba*, its symbols were no longer exotic. I knew the landscape from which they were taken, the tree and animal species used, the agricultural cycles

---

[1] A fairly full account of the symbolism of this ritual drama appears in Turner, *Revelation and Divination in Ndembu Ritual* (Ithaca, N.Y.: Cornell Univ. Press, 1975).

and hunting experiences to which they referred. More than that I knew the people using them as I have never really known people before or since that time of first field work—which for anthropologists is akin to the period of heightened sensibility we call "first love" or first anything else of our youth. The basic facts of human sociality, in its health and pathology, are the same everywhere. Ritual and literature, in their different ways (and we'll discuss the *how* of that difference later), provided what it is now fashionable to call "metalanguages" for discussing sociality, special ways of talking about general ways of talking and acting. To be technical, a metalanguage, as a language used to make assertions about another language, is any language whose symbols refer to the properties of the symbols of another language. Ritual and literature, in a way, are society talking about itself, the reflexivity of society. Yet, paradoxically, ritual language is less discursive and more condensed and cryptic, certainly more potent than ordinary language. Condensation occurs in ritual partly because ritual is society, not one of its components, talking; its speech is thick speech, dense with the past and a distillation of all contemporary social modes. Ritual is also society evaluating itself; out of its rich, deep experience it asserts that some things, for example, relationships, actions, thoughts, ideas, images, styles, are "good," others are "bad," others neutral or not yet fully appraised. Not all ritual is religious ritual, but religious ritual is not only society talking about itself but also talking about what transcends it, about God. As Sally Moore has recently written of aspects of classification in Chagga ritual symbolism ("The Well-Stitched Anus: A Fiction of Chagga Initiation and its Relation to the Logic of

Chagga Symbolism," unpublished paper, March 1975, p. 27):
"Part of the message of these (ritual) symbols is that there is an
underlying riddle that cannot be rationally solved, a riddle
about the source and meaning of life . . . Comprehensible limited surface orders and underlying unfathomable riddles about
meaning and relationship may be the very things that are being
represented." In Christian terms rituals insist upon saving
truths that transcend but do not deny rationality: on the paradox of infinity becoming finite, of the Creator becoming part of
Creation, of God dying, of the body being resurrected. These
issues of paradox beset the piece of field material I shall now
present.

   Almost at the end of the *Chihamba* ritual a personal shrine is
made a short distance from the doorway of each candidate's hut.
The process of constructing this shrine and the articles composing it make up a resumé of many features of Ndembu life and
culture. More than this they speak to us, too, once the ritual
idiom has been grasped. It must be understood that on the
previous day the candidates have symbolically slain an image of
Kavula made from a wooden framework covered by a brilliantly
white blanket. The "head" of the demigod is represented by an
inverted wooden meal mortar containing a bundle of symbolic
objects. While some adepts prepare this structure, others chase
the candidates—naked save for a waist-cloth—back and forth
along the path leading to the sacred enclosure with the image to
the senior candidate's house. Songs indicate that the candidates
have become slaves of *Kavula* and they carry symbolic slave
yokes. With each chasing they are brought ever nearer to *Kavula*'s tabernacle until, at sundown, they are brought up indi-

vidually and serially to make obeisance before the white image of the demideity. They are told to strike it "on the head" with special ceremonial rattles, and then that they have killed him. While "dying" the image shakes violently and finally keels over. Soon afterwards the candidates are told that they are innocent and that he is not dead, and the paraphernalia under the white cloth are revealed to be no more than some everyday implements—although for adepts each item has multiple meanings. Everyone then laughs joyfully. There is a live sense of *communitas,* a deep accord among adepts and candidates, eliminating distinctions of age, sex, village affiliation, rank, status, or role. One might say that a "social construction of reality" has been shown to be such that the candidates are relieved to have slain, not the god, but a symbolic means of portraying and thinking about him. The irony of the situation is that what seems a *deception* reveals a *truth,* that the act of being cannot be caught in cognitive nets, or adequately presented in symbols.

The following morning the god returns, but in a different way. He is now aligned more closely with nature than with culture. At the same time, it is now the turn for the individual candidate. On the day of chasing and apparent deicide, the candidates appeared as a collectivity; now each is singled out as a separate person and assigned a shrine of his or her own. On the first day, the ritual movement was oscillant but ultimately centripetal—all converge to destroy the image of the god and thus assert his reality, his act-of-being. On the second day, the ritual movement is centrifugal. The god who drew people to him now scatters himself among the single individuals. On the first day, the movement between tabernacle and home culminated at the tabernacle, as a cultural artifact. On the second day, the ritual focus is on the home; the invisible god comes to private shrines and is there embodied in the seeds of edible crops. Before, the many came to the one; now the one comes to the many. Encompassing both is the ritual process which expresses the paradox that the one is the many and the many are one.

The ritual itself, like most Ndembu rituals, is performed with and through simple material things and simple actions and gestures. Their significance is not so simple, however, as we shall see, though it will be accessible to us. My contention has always been, in various writings, that a truly rendered reflexive statement about any isolable natural process of human experience—whether individual or social—consolidates into a sequence and patterning of symbols, each of which is multivocal (susceptible of many meanings) and which together represent a statement of the problems, partial solutions, and abiding paradoxes of the human condition.

Early, then, on the second day, the candidates are taken to a species of tree called *Ikamba daChihamba,* literally a "cassava" or "manioc-root" of *Chihamba* (from its swollen shape). A senior female adept bares the white taproot of this tree, which is said to represent, nay to *"be," Kavula,* the god slain previously in effigy. Then a senior male adept cuts off a branch of the root; and this, together with other symbolic vegetable objects, is taken back to the village. Here again, this episode is said to be a "wounding" of *Kavula* and unguents are applied to the root wherever it has been cut by the adept's hoe. There is something akin to the Western theological notion of transubstantiation here; the "substance" of the root is the deity *Kavula,* its "accidents" are its natural properties. On their way back to the village the 'adepts stop to draw a white clay image of *Kavula* (like a cross) on the ground. They conceal this under a medicine basket and make a double arch at its foot with a split sapling. The candidates are made to crawl up to the image and greet it as they greeted the forest image on the previous day. But now it is their turn to be symbolically killed. *Kavula* acting through his officiants ceremonially beheads them by passing a knife over their shoulders. Dialecticians might see in this concrete logic a kind of "negation of the negation." *Kavula*'s "death" is cancelled by the candidates' "death." Life, health, and fertility can now prevail. Death is dead.

Back in the village, the final important step is the setting-up, for each candidate, of a personal shrine, known as *Kantong'a,* to the *Chihamba* spirits, both god and ancenstress. These will henceforth be sources of benefit to their former victims. The setting-up of shrines begins with that of the senior female candidate, she who was first afflicted and whose house on the previous day represented one symbolic pole of the ritual process. *Kavula*'s tabernacle represented the whole land against her particular home, fertility in general against her specific reproductive power, the bush against the domestic sphere, hunting masculinity against cultivating and procreant feminity, health against illness, and many other oppositions. Now the meaning and power of the whole ritual are being incorporated in the new shrines constructed not within but just outside the houses of the candidates.

To make such a shrine a bundle of twigs cut from trees that are symbolic not only of *Chihamba* spirits but also of other modes of affliction is thrust into a hole and tamped with cool, stream-bottom black mud. Sacralized white maize beer is then poured on it as a libation. A clay pot containing medicine made from the bark and leaves of the species from which the twigs were taken is placed near the bundle, and the blood of a decapitated white hen is poured into it, the severed head being placed on the apex of the bundle and the intestines draped around the twigs. A senior male adept then digs a circle in the earth round the shrine with the butt of his sacred, personal rattle. Beans and maize grains are then planted in the trench by all the adepts in unison. A section of the *ikamba daChihamba* root, representing *Kavula,* is partially buried near the pot on the side nearest to the candidate's hut. Libations are poured at each end of the root. Lines are then drawn in white manioc meal from the medicine pot and root to the doorway of the hut and also to the shrine trees planted to the village ancestors. In this way the suspicious power of the *Chihamba* ritual is channelled to where it can do most good. While these actions are being performed the senior male adept invokes the spirits of *Chihamba,* and now he uses the candidate's new cultic name, for she has been transformed into an adept.

Every item, every gesture, has significance at *Kantong'a.* Ndembu ritual symbols are what semioticians call "iconic:" an icon entails similarity between signifier and signified. This seems to have nothing in common with "icon" in the Christian tradition, but is an idiolect usage of the philosopher Charles S. Pierce. An icon is a type of sign, and, since the Stoics, a sign is thought of as made up of two halves, one sensible, one intelligible: the "signifier," a perceptible impact on at least one of the sense organs of the interpreter; and the content signified. Charles Morris speaks of the signifier (medieval Latin, *signans*) as the "sign vehicle" and the signified (medieval Latin, *signatum*) as the "designatum." Saussure uses the terms *"significant"* and *"signifié."* Let us look at the bundle of twigs which forms a central part of the personal shrine. Each species of tree is an iconic sign or symbol. In Ndembu ritual iconicity has three main forms: nominal, substantial, and artifactual. Put simply, an icon's meaning is derived from its name, its nature, and its fashioning by human activity. Thus the name of an object used in ritual may be connected by folk etymology to the name or part of a name denoting some other object, activity, relationship, conception, or quality. We shall see how this works in a moment. The natural properties of an object, whether it is a gas, a liquid, or a solid; animal, vegetable or mineral; plain, striped, or spotted; its color, texture, taste, smell, sound, location, habitus, normal setting, and many more—one or several of these may be selected as foundations for meaning. Finally, a natural object may be worked upon by purposive human activity and shaped into an artifact. This additional cultural elaboration then becomes a further basis of meaning.

Let's begin at the "nominal" end of this semantic spectrum. The names of the trees from which twigs are taken are, in order of collection: *mudyi, mukula, musoli, mukombukombu, mututambululu,* and *muhotuhotu.* The prefix *mu-*, pl. *nyi,* commonly applies to the class of trees and shrubs in Ndembu ethnobotany.

None of my informants connected *mudyi* with another

Ndembu word or radical, but I have reason to believe that the radical *dyi-* is derived from *dya,* "eat." This would be consistent with its substantial basis, as we shall see.

All Ndembu link *mukula* with *kula,* "to pass a culturally defined point of maturity," such as the transition from childhood to social maturity, or from middle age to elderhood. Roughly, it means "to grow up, mature." Its primary denotation is the onset of the menses in a girl.

Many Ndembu, especially adepts in the various kinds of ritual cults which use it, derive *musoli* from *ku-solola,* "to produce to view, make visible, manifest."

Mukombukombu is derived by informants from *ku-komba,* "to sweep," which is itself connected by them with *ku-kombela,* "to invoke spirits, to pray."

Mututambululu is associated by informants with *ambululu,* a species of small bee which hovers in clouds around the blossoms of this plant.

Muhotuhotu, according to some informants, is from *ku-hotumuna,* "to fall at once," said of leaves falling together from a shaken tree, and to others, from *ku-hotumuka,* "to slip and fall"—one informant added, "like a windfallen tree lodged on another one, so a sickness *(musong'u)* lies on a patient's body; they (adepts) want to make it slip off *(hotumuka).*"

At the level of "substantial" iconicity, *mudyi* is a tree which when cut secretes a white milky latex. I have discussed its semantics in many books and articles. Like all dominant ritual symbols it is susceptible of many meanings. Among these are motherhood, womanhood, matriliny, a particular matrilineage, the mother-child bond, lactation, the learning process, and so on, all derived by association or analogy (that is, in an iconic fashion) from the tree's natural property of exuding white fluid which closely resembles the way beads of milk emerge from a mother's nipple. In *Chihamba,* a further designation of *mudyi* is deemed important: since this tree is used in primary rites of passage, such as the girl's puberty ritual and the boys' circumcision ritual as a dominant symbol, it is used metonymically for initiation.

Mukula, like *mudyi,* also secretes gum. But this gum is red and thick, not white and fine. Ndembu compare it with blood, calling it "the blood of the *mukula* tree." In their ritual taxonomy there are different categories of blood, as I have shown elsewhere: blood of childbirth, menstrual blood, blood of circumcision, blood of hunting, blood of homicide, and blood of witchcraft (for witches are believed to be necrophagous cannibals). The *mukula* tree and *mukula* gum may be contextually specified to mean any of these. The gum's propensity to coagulate is stressed in some cases; for example, in cults to cure women's reproductive disorders, *mukula* is used to make the menstrual blood, running away uselessly, cohere to form a fetus and placenta, and in boys' circumcision, to cause the operation wound to scab over. *Mukula* like *mudyi* in *Chihamba* is an index of initiation; its very name, as we have seen, means to pass a point of maturation.

The other three species are usually found together in Ndembu ritual, for their branches or twigs are literally bound together in many rites to form a broom (*chisampu*) used for splashing or sweeping the patient (candidate) with medicine prepared from pounded leaves, bark scrapings, or root parings of ritually significant species. Here we are already dealing with the artifactual basis of meaning, but this is unavoidable. A medicine broom is said by informants to "sweep away diseases" or "sweep away the familiars of witchcraft." But it also contains the positive implication of something swept *on* as well. This is iconically connected with the fact that all three trees have large nectar-filled flowers attractive to bees—as we have seen, the name of one of them is derived from a species of bee. Sweeping with the three-stranded *chisampu* is thought to make the patient "attractive," to draw many people to the rites, and thus "add power" to them. Again, women so swept will have many children, a hunter will kill many animals, many will praise the patient. Thus the medicine broom indicates the process it expedites. It purifies from pollution by its sweeping and *eo ipso* creates for the patient an auspicious ritual condition which will draw towards it much success, many benefits, and popularity.

All five tree species are found in many kinds of Ndembu ritual. In some rituals one or another is a dominant or focal symbol about which their entire symbolic repertoire is grouped. Together they constitute the ensemble of the highest, most pervasive values explicitly recognized in Ndembu culture, as well as the lowest common denominators of biological, domestic, and economic experience.

The artifactual basis of meaning may be seen (a) in the tying of the twigs into a bundle; and (b) in the position of the bundle vis-a-vis other components of the personal *Kantong'a* shrine. (a) The bundle is a compendium of Ndembu cults of affliction. (b) My informants told me that the *ikela* or hole in which it was placed made it stand upright, for standing up means strength for the candidate. The *malowa,* black river mud, "is cool, for it comes from water. It is put in the hole so that all the diseases and troubles in the bundle should rest peacefully forever after. For the bundle (*kaseli*) is a collection of every disease that attacked the candidate (*muyeji*) into one form." Water, too, is often used as an initiatory symbol (just as we use it in baptism).

If the bundle is an epitome of "all the ills that flesh is heir to," the horizontally placed root of *ikamba daChihamba,* representing the demigod *Kavula,* stands for the singularity of the candidate, for her or his specific relationship to the deity. It also indicates the contrapuntal character of *Chihamba* in relation to all other Ndembu cults. Its half-buried character, said my best informant, Muchona, "means that you only saw the back of *Kavula* as he came out of the ground." This refers also to the image of *Kavula* in the tabernacle on the previous day. *Kavula* is at once a sky-god or weather-god and an earth-god or vegetation-god. His name, as I said, is an archaic term for the lightning of the rainy season and is connected with *nvula,* which with its cognates in almost all Bantu languages means rain. I have shown elsewhere (*Chihamba the White Spirit,* 1962; *Revelation and Divination in Ndembu Ritual,* 1975), that *Kavula* is also symbolically connected with thunder, with hunting, with the sound of firearms, with high authority, with grandparenthood, and especially with white symbolism, which is at once a sign of the ancestral spirits and of auspiciousness. He is also a sign of transformation: he dies as rain to become crops and food. Hence the circle of grains and, I should add, the cutting of manioc planted around the bundle of medicine twigs. Those initiated into his cult are transformed too; they partake of his numinos-

ity, of the immense concentration of sometimes disparate powers and meanings brought together in the symbolic vehicles of
his cult and finally deposited in the *Kantong'a* shrine. *Kantong'a*
itself means "a memorial," for Ndembu derive it from *ku-
tong'ashana*, "to think about," perhaps even to "meditate upon."
It is a living reminder of *Kavula*, whose name must never be
mentioned aloud in the mundane world or to those uninitiated
in his cult. When the grains and beans, which are supposed to
be a compendium of all Ndembu food crops, have grown to a
reasonable height, food taboos laid on the candidates are lifted.
The taboos concern mostly striped or spotted animals, fish, or
birds, for their marks resemble those made by leprosy, and the
sanction against breaking the rules of *Chihamba* is affliction by
this disease, itself the negative power of whiteness, *Kavula's*
color.

There is nothing about these patterns of symbolic objects and
actions which we can truthfully say is really alien to our own
way of experiencing life. All the big issues are here expressed:
life / death; sickness / health; male / female; individual / community;   familiar / strange;   nature / culture;   purification / pollution; the personal crisis that may lead to individua-
tion; the overcoming of conflict to revitalize social cohesion.
Local features do abound, of course. There is the contrast not of
summer, fall, winter, and spring, but between dry and wet
seasons—with great *Kavula*-like storms on the threshold of the
rains. There is the overweening presence of the savannah, the
deciduous woodland, broken intermittently by grassy plains,
the frailty of the wattle-and-daub huts in which people live.

There is the necessity of surviving on what one grows, hunts, collects, and.fishes for, not on what one buys. There is relatively rudimentary technology; hoes not ploughs, no cattle or horses for food or traction. There is a high rate of infant mortality and a low rate of life expectancy for all. Society is disease-logged; malaria, bilharzia, yaws, hookworm, sleeping sickness, relapsing fever, tuberculosis, and many others. Relationships among kinsfolk are close and continuous; some have political value. Thus men succeed to office and inherit wealth through the mother's, not the father's, side of the family. If you're a headman, your sister's son, not your own son, will succeed to your position and inherit your muzzle-loading gun, if you're lucky enough to have one. Property is simple and mostly movable. Indeed, with shifting cultivation and hunting, the tiny villages themselves pull up stakes and move on every five years or so. There are other major differences from life as we experience it in an industrialized, urban milieu, conscious of millennia of written history and literature, and often abiding among the huge only slowly perishing artifacts and buildings of our predecessors. But members of a species which has been able to adapt to all kinds of climatic, geographical, and social conditions, whose members learn many new roles in the course of their lives, whose cultural outputs are almost infinitely varied, can easily slip into the skins of Ndembu and see how they use their environment as a source of symbolic forms for experiences all human beings share.

Even the purely religious aspects of *Chihamba* have an oddly familiar ring for Westerners. There is a deity who is slain by his people, is resurrected, and produces life more abundantly. One recalls the Biblical verse: "Unless a grain of wheat falls to the ground and dies, it remains only a single grain; but if it dies, it yields a rich harvest" (Gospel according to St. John xii.24). By entering into the death of their deity, candidates are reborn (the symbolism is clear) as members of his cultus and receive new names in religion. The deity comes from the sky, and by his death renews the earth. He is connected with whiteness and water and supreme authority. He heals the afflicted. There is no doubt that *Chihamba* is a traditional Ndembu ritual that has not been affected by missionary influences from the West.

II

We must now consider whether it is possible to analyse symbols in Western literature in the same way and to compare the results with those obtained in studying tribal ritual symbols. One problem is that literature is a matter of the written word, and writing imposes a linear and hierarchical form, while ritual is act and process and may have several vortices of ritual action going on at the same time—like a three-ring circus. Literary forms relate to earlier literary forms, and no two works are closely similar. Rituals are transmitted orally and often learnt in their practice, not from books. But there are deeper differences, and it is to these that I would like to call your attention. Recently I have been giving tutorials in the Committee on Social Thought at the University of Chicago on Dante, Blake, and Kierkegaard. My method of approach to their texts—and on the Committee we always go directly to texts, probe them as far as we can, and only then seek help from commentators—is to treat them as sequences of multivocal symbols.

In the Dante tutorial, for example, we approached the first canto of the *Purgatorio* as if it were the account of a ritual process given us by an exceptionally gifted native informant. We listed all the objects, proper nouns, persons, actions, relationships, attributes, topographical features, and so on, which could be shown to have a symbolic value, that is, in addition to its denotation to designate a number of other objects, conceptions, religious doctrines, etc., beyond their literal sense. At first we tried to elucidate Dante by Dante; we looked for exegetical help from other parts of the *Commedia,* or from other works of Dante, such as the *Vita Nuova,* the *Convivio,* and *De Monarchia.* Then we invoked the help of commentators, such as Charles Singleton, Arnaldo Momigliano, Dorothy Sayers, Umberto Cosmo, Ernst Curtius, and others. From such varied sources, the following schema emerged for the first book. As we shall see, an initiation scenario emerges which is comparable with the episode of *Kantong'a* in the Ndembu ritual. Here Virgil and Cato are the adepts, while Dante the pilgrim—not to be confused here with Dante the poet-narrator—is the candidate. He is to be symbolically purified and humbled before he can ascend the mountain of Purgatory on his way to Paradise. Dante's book, of course, like the *Chihamba* ritual emerged from a situation of social conflict: the poet was exiled by his political opponents, the Black Guelphs of Florence. I shall not burden you with a heap of particular symbols—it took us a whole term to work our way through the first short canto—but will focus on a few relevant to the initiation theme. And, incidentally, I hope to show the virtues of structuralism as a mode of description and ordering of textual materials, if not as a general theory of mind and culture.

The Processual Form of Canto I of the Purgatorio

Canto I begins with nautical symbols—Dante's little humble boat elevates its sails, leaving a cruel sea, Inferno, for better waters, Purgatorio. The notion of elevation, breeze to fill the sails, movement in a favorable element, become prominent. There is also the notion of resurrection, "dead poetry rise again," Muses breathe inspiration into the sails, now, however, as "sacred Muses," pagan goddesses baptized and transformed, a nature good enough for grace to build on. The resurrection theme, associated with female powers, is enhanced by the reference to the Muses' song celebrating Persephone who rose from the dead after immersion in the night of Hades, against the perverse song of the piebald magpie Pierides, who suppose the earth giants to have overthrown the heavenly gods, putting Below where Above should be. In fact, the true course is ever upward, from Hell up to Purgatory, then up the Mountain of Purgatory, where the ascent gets easier the higher one climbs, to Heaven and its successive circles which go up to the Beatific Vision of the Trinity. But since Man has fallen in his originally created nature he has to be recreated or regenerated. Hence the descent of figures such as Beatrice (prefigured by the myth of Persephone) and especially God Himself in his Second Person, who harrowed Hell, or rather Limbo, to raise fallen souls like Dante first to the Earthly Paradise of Natural Perfection on the top of the Purgatorial Mountain, then to the true supernatural Heaven. Even Virgil is raised from Limbo to the Earthly Paradise before he must relinquish Dante to the guidance of Beatrice. And Christ raised Cato from Limbo to be the guardian of the Mountain of Purgatory, not a jailer like Minos over the Inferno, but a liberator urging souls onward and upward towards the earthly and heavenly Paradises.

After the water and breath imagery of sea and Muses, we have a set of Ptolemaic astronomical and astrological images, in which the South represents the unfallen world, the North the fallen world, the Southern Cross the Four Cardinal Virtues (shared by pagans and Christians), where Venus, mother of the true principle of Roman *monarchia*, represented by Virgil's Augustinian age and his prophecy of the return of a Golden Age, anticipates the coming of the Sun, the true Christian God; just as Beatrice, Matelda, and other female figures are later to lead Dante to the true Christian heaven. The Fishes veiled by the Love Planet may be not only the constellation Pisces, but also the Fish symbol for Christ, used in the catacombs by the first persecuted Christians. Sea and sky produce a sort of baptism of the Roman principle of Monarchia in its Utopian Virgilian form.

Cato, the Mediator, then comes into prominence. He stands between Hell, from which he was taken by Christ, and Purgatory proper. He knows the "laws of the abyss" which separate Hell and Purgatory. On the one side, or rather *below,* is a heap of dark symbols: "dead air, blind stream, eternal prison, deep night, black infernal valley, evil stream, defilement." On the other is the open sky, where the light of the four holy stars representing the four cardinal virtues, Justice, Prudence, Fortitude, and Temperance makes Cato's face shine "as if the sun (of Christian truth) were before him." His true realm is the *limen* of the shore of the little island on which the great mountain is perched. But he separates Hell from Purgatory and cannot be won by Virgil's appeal to his love for his wife; a great gulf now separates Cato and Marcia.

Cato has much body symbolism—white-streaked beard, a double tress of hair (to express his duality?), a bright face, eyes that were once pleased by Marcia, a "holy breast" (possibly a reference to Lucan's *Pharsalia* IX. 561–62, *"Tua pectora sacra / Voce reple,"* "Fill your breast with the sacred utterance [of the god]").

Virgil, instigated by Cato, then involves Dante in a good deal of body symbolism also. Before that he had "laid hold on me, and with speech and hand and sign made reverent my legs and brow," that is, made Dante bow his head and kneel before the virtuous Roman. Then, on Cato's instructions, Virgil led Dante back a little in the Hell-ward direction, signifying humility, or *reculer pour mieux sauter* perhaps to a place where the breeze preserved the dew (perhaps a symbol of God's grace) from evaporation by the sun. Then he performs a kind of ritual which seems to combine the functions of purificatory ablution (ridding Dante of the sooty stains of Hell which hide his true "color" and baptising him into a new, more hopeful life). The cincture, made of a rush with which Virgil girds Dante, reminds us that a rush or reed was one of St. John the Baptist's attributes in medieval iconography. It was also, of course, a rush that was put in the hand of Jesus as a mock-sceptre after he had been scourged at the Pillar. Again, the fact that another rush springs up to replace the one taken clearly betokens rebirth and resurrection and their association with humility, the dominant mood of Purgatory.

This whole episode has clear Virgilian echoes, literally so, since they come from the *Aeneid*. For example, when Aeneas, in Book VI, 635–36, leaves black Tartarus and enters the Elysian fields: *"Occupat Aeneas aditum corpusque recenti spargit aqua ramumque in limine figit"* (Aeneas wins the entrance, sprinkles his body with fresh water, and plants the bough full on the threshold). In the *Purgatorio,* Dante causes Virgil himself to treat Dante, the pilgrim, as a Christian Aeneas, sacralizing him to enter a pure realm. Note the literally "liminal" state of both Aeneas and Virgil.

Lévi-Strauss would be delighted by the binary oppositions disclosed in the topography of Purgatory, in its relation to other domains of the cosmos, and in its internal structure, in this first canto. There is the opposition between sea and island, between sky and earth, between left and right, between up and down, between the enclosed domain of Hell and the open domain of Purgatory, between (Cato's) rocks and the ("soft mud" of the) shore, between the northern and southern hemispheres, between the upperworld (the mountain of Purgatory) and the underworld (the Inferno), and (implicitly) between the East with its "oriental sapphire" of sunrise and the West (which we will learn is sundown when no more activity is possible on the Mountain until the next dawn), and between the "solitary plain" around the mountain's base and (as we shall learn) the much-peopled terraces of the purgatorial mountain. Finally, when one looks East, at sunrise, South, to the night, the suspicious side, and North to the left, the inauspicious side.

Further Structuralist Conjectures

Topography is perhaps the most accessible aspect of symbolism to structuralist procedure in the Roman Jakobson–Lévi-Strauss tradition, but while we are on the matter, further binary contrasts might be drawn here. In the temporal order we have— in terms of earlier and later—the Venus–Sun dichotomy, the Cato–Virgil relationship (Cato = the best of the Republic, Virgil produced the ideal model for Monarchia), the Virgil–Dante opposition, pagan versus Christian epic poet; then there is the Pierides–Muses competition, which corresponds to the Giants–Gods conflict, which corresponds to the rebellion of local particularism against the generic, universalistic principle of Monarchia (for Dante, the modernization process which would overcome local segmentation of Christendom).

At the level of sex symbolism we have the Virgil–Beatrice complementarity, in which a Christian representative of the weaker sex (in terms of both Roman and medieval patriarchal systems) commands (and in terms of the symbolic actions we considered there can hardly be any other interpretation—"I was sent to him to rescue him," and so on). In a sense, this is a reversal of the pagan Roman evaluation of the directions. Robert Hertz, for example, in his classical essay "The Preeminence of the Right Hand" (in R. Needham's translation), writes: "For the Hindus and the Romans the north is the *regio fausta* (the happy, fortunate region) and inhabited by the gods while the

South belongs to the dead." Dante keeps the South for the purgatorial dead, but makes it also a *regio fausta*. Dante's ideal Roman pagan poet, philosopher, and ideologue of benevolent imperialism comes to rescue Dante from the servitude of sins which gave him "little time left to run." Here we have the dichotomy above–below, with the rule that "above is better" operating. Also the dichotomy Christian woman–pagan man, with the implication that a structurally inferior female is superior to a structurally superior male in terms of Christian theology. Here, too, we have the notion that the Kingdom of Heaven of the parables is really a sort of *un*-kingdom, in which the weak or structurally inferior are saved—this accords well with the general theme of humility or self-accepted humiliation which is the *leit-motiv* of the *Purgatorio*. I cite in support of this view such symbolic objects as "little ship," "little island," "little grass," "humble plant," "soft rushes," "tear-stained cheeks," "dew in the breeze," which for a while resists the drying power of the heat, and such symbolic actions as Dante's bowing before Cato and accepting Virgil's act of cincturing him with a reed girdle. The theme that the historically "later is better" is concretized not only in the Venus–Sun, matins–dawn temporal order, but also in the Marcia–Beatrice comparison. Cato is "moved no more" by Marcia, because she dwells "beyond the evil stream," that is, in a downward direction, in the *Inferno*, even though, in that dread realm, she is in the Limbo of the good pagans. But Virgil, himself from Limbo, and therefore, in a way, inferior in state to Cato, *is* induced by Beatrice's prayers, "a lady descended from Heaven," to come to the rescue of the almost damned Dante—damned perhaps through lust and pride. Christian "paradoxes" abound here: in the secular-cultural anti-logic of this frame; woman is better than man, another man's wife (Beatrice) is better than one's own wife (Cato), *above* is humility (heaven approached by the Purgatorial mountain) *below* is pride (Hell), Virgil (though from the *Inferno*) ascends higher than Cato (who has been released by Christ's "harrowing of hell" from the "laws of the abyss"), yet Cato will eventually attain heaven while Virgil will not. Before one may mount one must be abased: the cincture of rushes, the descent to the shore of the "little island" on which there stands such a huge mountain. In Dante's Christian scheme humility rises, pride sinks. Or, perhaps, we might say, with St. Francis de Sales, that "love is humility rising, while humility is love descending."

Some Dantean Paradoxes: Beatrice–Marcia

But as we have often had occasion to note, there remain some paradoxes of Dante's own. These often concern the nature of the relationship between pagan Roman and various Christian figures and ideas. What, for example, are we to make of the relationship between Dante–Beatrice and Cato–Marcia? In the former case, Dante, for whatever reason, failed to marry an idealized woman, who married another and died young without children; but who, in his imagination, posthumously descended from heaven to save her lover (whom, living, she is not known to have loved equally) from damnation. In the latter case, Cato married Marcia when she was young—she was his second, not his first wife—and she bore him three children. After that, Cato gave her to his friend Hortensius, to whom she also bore children, fruit of her obedience to the stern Cato. When Hortensius died, in Lucan's words, "wearied and worn out with child-bearing" she returned to Cato, and implored him: "Grant me to renew the faithful compact of my first marriage; grant me only the name of wife; suffer men to write on my tomb, 'Marcia, wife of Cato' " (*Phars.* II.338–44). We have here a classic case of Lévi-Straussian "structural inversion." The idealized and fantasized Beatrice tries after death to save the man she did not marry, Dante; the real and rejected Marcia tries before death to save her own marriage to a husband who had given her away. Beatrice, who, if we are to believe the *Vita Nuova,* once jested with her friends at Dante's expense, had no children; Marcia who always took Cato very much in earnest, bore him and his friend children. There is another thread to the story, of course. Dante was for a time by his own confession highly unfaithful to Beatrice's memory; Cato, although he "put Marcia away" was virtuous in all ways. But Dante puts Cato now in the vestibule of Purgatory, awaiting heaven, hence, with hope, above Marcia, who exists without hope but also without pain, in Limbo, while Beatrice is above Cato stationed at a high level of Heaven, and above Dante, although he hopes to reach heaven eventually through Beatrice's aid. Yet Cato will also reach heaven after the Last Judgment, according to the text we have just read. It may or may not be significant that Dante mentions in his poem neither Beatrice's husband, Simone de'Bardi, a member of one of the great banking houses of Florence, nor Marcia's second husband Hortensius, Cato's friend. What is Dante trying to say, then? Is it, in the language of inversion, a message that first love is best love, and that just as Cato received Marcia back in marriage at the pagan level of virtuous earthly life, so will Bea-

trice receive Dante back in non-marriage at the level of heavenly
life, which is a life of grace not natural virtue? But in the af-
terlife, Cato "may no more be moved" by Marcia, "now that she
dwells beyond the evil stream," in Limbo, beyond Acheron,
"the river of pain or woe," while Beatrice "moves and directs"
not only Virgil, but also Dante, as we shall see, and moves him
towards the Beatific Vision. Perhaps, here, the Christian doctrine that "in heaven, there is neither marriage nor giving in
marriage," but instead, the infinite and generous reciprocity of
all souls, is a factor in Dante's argument.

I have already discussed the paradoxical position of Cato,
pagan, suicide, and putter-away of a virtuous wife, who caused
her to bear children in adultery according to Christian standards. The roles of the female pagan deities, Venus and the
Muses, in a Christian didactic-cum-epic poem have also been
mentioned.

Now let us go back to themes detectable in the symbol
vehicles. One can, for example, array symbols under the pagan–
Christian contrast. Pagan symbols would include: muses, Cal-
liope, Pierides, Venus, Fishes, Wain, Cato, Marcia, the evil
stream, Virgil, Minos. Christian symbols would include: Hell,
Purgatory, Heaven, lady of heaven, Beatrice, Dante, rush, humility, angel, breeze (of grace), sun, little island, grass, boat,
and so on, matina, purificatory washing, resurrection of the
body (1.75), four stars, first people, and so on. There are also
ambiguous symbols: "sacred" Muses, Cato (pagan freedom from
tyranny and Christian freedom from sin), the Sun (as both
Apollo, god of medicine, music, and prophecy, and the Christian God), Dante's act of obeisance to Cato as both a pagan act

of filial piety and a Christian genuflection to a *figura* of God the Father (as Dante himself states in the *Convivio* IV.xxviii.15–19, when he says that Marcia's return to Cato after Hortensius' death symbolizes the noble soul returning to God in old age).

III

This Christian–pagan contrast, ambiguity, and tension stresses the difference between African ritual and European literature. For the *literatus* is working in a culture of papyrus and vellum, later of paper and printing, in which descriptions, observations, commentaries, and interpretations of the world have been accumulated over the centuries, and to which he has access. The composers of tribal rituals—and there are innovative geniuses of liturgy too—work in oral traditions in which precise historical time depth is relatively shallow and becomes blended with mythical thought and imagery. Dante had time, in his long exile, to ruminate over Christian and pagan written works and documents. They could be embodied into his subjectivity, his inwardness. If they raised problems for him, these very problems could be ventilated in poetic forms which themselves were products of literary traditions. For the tribal ritual "artists" their creations came out of the heat, the "effervescence," Durkheim might have said, of intersubjective, corporate action, forming themselves like the motifs and phrases of jazz musicians in the crucible of the living event. Live communion generated metaphors and symbols of its own sensuous incarnation.

Tribal rituals are conceived of as "work" and have a central place in cultural dynamics. The whole society participates in life

crisis rituals, in calendrical feasts, and everyone undergoes therapeutic ritual at some time in life. It is obligatory to pass
through major initiations. But in an advanced phase of the
division of labor, the domain of religion itself has contracted
and is occupied by a plurality of churches and sects. Moreover,
ritual itself has become an issue; some religious groups eschew it
on principle, others water it down. With the contraction of the
religious domain and its relegation for the masses of the surviving "faithful" to the sphere of leisure "time offs," many of its
former attributes have been secularized and have then themselves fallen under the influence of the division of labor. In
Ndembu ritual, for example, what we would call art, music,
sculpture, poetry, and drama are all strands of ritual action. In
Western European Culture, with nodal points of change at the
Renaissance, Reformation, and Industrial Revolution, these aesthetic processes have become increasingly specialized, secularized, diverse, individualized, voluntarized, and controversial.
These, too, belong mainly to leisure, particularly as regards
their consumption. Individuals generate art works—which often
become commodities on the market—out of freedom and subjectivity. Thus Dante's vision was by no means the *Summa poe-
tica* of medieval culture (equivalent to St. Thomas' *Summa theo-
logica*) it has often been held to be. It was often a somewhat
subversive metasocial commentary on politics, religion, contemporary morality, and current poetic practice in a changing liminal age—as perhaps might have been expected from a political exile who was strongly critical of the forms of government of
the Italian city state produced by the new merchant-aristocrats
and of the role of the Church in its dealings with the Empire,

the French monarchy, and the Italian city states. Ndembu ritual often contains what we would call "ludic" (playful) or joking episodes. Sometimes its symbols portray reversal of the normal social and political structure. But this merely relates to experiences of the cyclical, repetitive character of the universe, of life and death, of village growth and decay. The reversive is not the potentially subversive. Again the focal ethical unit is the corporate group of kin, not the single individual. Though *Chihamba* does in fact give greater weight to individual destiny than most Ndembu rituals, it is still mostly performed as a remedy against social conflict in the interest of the wider community.

With all these differences go many similar features. Both rituals and literary works are highly complex semiotic phenomena. Both are systems of multivocal or polysemous signs (symbols). In both cases the symbols concentrate and bring within a single limited context many designations that are in ordinary life scattered widely through the events of each day and year in the lives of individuals and societies. As Barbara Babcock-Abrahams has recently written of the relation between ritual and the novel: "Just as ritual may combine and recapitulate the cultural repertoire of performance types and communicative relationships, so the novel is sufficiently flexible and 'open' that it may introduce the different voices of any and all other literary genres, not to mention extra-literary ones." [2] Both ritual and literary opus are metalanguages, in the former case a nonverbal as well as verbal one, confronting in their symbolisms and within their frames,

[2] "The Novel and the Carnival World: An Essay in Memory of Joe Doherty," *Modern Language Notes,* 1975, p. 912.

forms and values that would otherwise be regarded as separate, discrepant, or even opposed. Dante confronts ancient Roman with contemporary Christian principles and practices. In *Chihamba* systems based on kinship are juxtaposed with systems based on territory and friendship. Both the poem and the ritual take stock of the cultures in which they are embedded and of which they constitute, so to speak, the reflecting mind and feeling heart. Since the symbol is the semantic molecule, the ultimate unit of specific structure, in both ritual and literary contexts, it is not surprising to find it a microcosm of the whole process or opus. That is why both Ndembu ritual symbol and Dantean poetic symbol share the following attributes:

1. multiple meanings (*signifiés*);

2. unification of disparate *signifiés*—essentially different signifieds are interconnected by analogy or by some link of association in fact or thought;

3. condensation—many ideas, relations between things, actions, interactions, and transactions are represented simultaneously by the symbol or icon vehicle (the ritual or poetic use of such a vehicle abridges what would otherwise be a lengthy verbal statement or argument);

4. polarization of signifieds—referents especially of dominant symbols tend often to be grouped at opposed semantic poles: one refers to components of the moral and social orders (the ideological or normative pole of meaning); the other (the sensory or orectic pole) refers to phenomena and processes that may be expected to arouse feelings and desires, including sexual, metabolic, aggressive, and work activities. Thus in *Chihamba*, the *ikamba daChihamba* root stands both for the

wounded body of a deity and all the virtues and values he
represents.

In Canto I of the Purgatorio the lines:

Lo bel pianeto che d'amar conforta
The fair planet that prompts to love
faceva tutto rider l'oriente
was making the whole East smile

exemplify all the attributes I have been assigning to dominant
symbols. It is at once a description of a satisfying visual experience, a reference to Venus and to the sunrise which its own rising as Morning star portended, a reference to classical mythology, especially to Virgil's poetry, and a condensed account of
Dante's own political ideology. For Venus was the mother of
Aeneas, whose Trojans were held to be ancestors of the Roman
people. *Venus genetrix* was venerated as mother of the Roman
people, especially of the Julian house, descended from Iulus,
grandson of Venus, whom the Iulii, following Cato's lead, identified with Ascanius, son of Aeneas. Julius Caesar belonged to
this house, as, of course, did Augustus Caesar, first emperor
who presided over the Augustan age which both Dante and
before him, Virgil, his psychopomp, admired. Virgil's famous
Fourth Eclogue written in 40 B.C. predicts the return of a
golden age, and a new-born child is to rule a pacified world
with the virtues of his father. Dante, like most educated Christians, supposed that Virgil, under divine inspiration, was refer-
ring to the dawn of the Christian era. Venus, heralding the
dawn was imperial, pacifying Rome, heralding the birth of

Christ. For Dante, the sun nearly always signifies God; as it is Easter morning when the poets emerge from the *Inferno* on to the shoreline of the island of Mount Purgatory, Venus now appears not only as precursor of Christ's Nativity but also of His Resurrection. At yet another level, Venus may be said to prefigure the coming of Dante's guide through heaven, Beatrice, who will take over Virgil's role of guide and teacher in the Earthly Paradise on the summit of the mountain. Venus means "charm" or "blooming nature;" her name may even be derived from *venia,* "the grace of the gods." [3]

The difference between Ndembu and European dominant symbols is not in their semantic structure but in the *oral* versus *written* traditions in which they are embedded. Venus, in Dante, has orectic and normative poles. Later, in Canto XXVII.94–96, he will write in passionate terms of the goddess who is a "planet" (and who in the *Paradiso* presides over the Third Heaven): "In the hour, I think, that from the east First shone from the mountain Cytherea, who with the fire of love (is) for ever burning." Dante knew well that the epithet "Cytherea" came from the island of Cythera, off the Peloponnesus, near which Venus rose from the foam of the sea. Here the erotic as well as maternal overtones of Venus are striking, linked to the opposite feminine qualities possessed by the blessed Beatrice and perhaps hinting at the presence of the Magdalene and other holy women at the Empty Tomb on Resurrection morning.

I have abundantly shown how Ndembu symbols, such as *mudyi,* the milk-tree, and *makula,* the blood-tree, have physio-

---

[3] Michael Grant, *Roman Myths* (New York: Scribner's, 1971), p. 65.

logical and ideological poles of meaning. It is my argument that it is through their dominant symbols or iconic signs, which constitute the molecules both of African ritual and European literature, that the action genres of the former and the written texts of the latter may best be compared. Dominant symbols provide the fixed points in the total systems, ritual or literary. They designate the major themes of the cultures for which they are supreme modes of expression. Sometimes they also embody critiques of those principles and values, or enunciate new, unprecedented themes. Analysis of dominant symbols and the clusters of ancillary symbols which they organize is perhaps the best way to reveal differences in the implicit postulates of dynamical cultural systems. It raises questions which determine the shape and style of further, broader-gauged comparative research.

JEROME MAZZARO

❧

The Fact of Beatrice in The Vita Nuova

I

A reader of *The Vita Nuova* is immediately struck by the presence of Beatrice. She appears first in Chapter II, already "in glory," as having been the source of the poet's sexual and moral awakening, and by the end of Chapter V, one is informed that he will receive no material unless it relates "to the theme of that most gracious lady." [1] The romantic screens, the suffering, the changes in Dante's character center on her, whose Christlike perfection is apparent at her birth when "all nine of the moving heavens were in perfect conjunction one with the other." Indeed, she is "the number nine"—the miracle of the Trinity multiplied by itself to effect her wonder. She is also a respected lady and a model of Christian character who repeatedly rescues the poet from error and, in Eternity, continues to act in his behalf. She displays generosity in Chapter III in her speaking to the young Dante, reverence in her demeanor in church (V), moral indignation in her refusals to condone promiscuous behavior (X, XXXIX), playfulness in her response to the poet's stunned silence at the wedding feast (XIV), and daughterly devotion in her sorrow at her father's death (XXII). Her designation as an audience for a number of the poems suggests, in addition,

---

[1] For the convenience of non-Italian readers, I have used Barbara Reynolds' translation of *La Vita Nuova* (Baltimore: Penguin Books, 1969).

some degree of learning. But in this "little book of memory,"
she is overwhelmingly *the* sensitive memory by which actions are
to be judged as harmonious or discordant and one major means
by which the validity of the work's biographical content is to be
evaluated.

The fact of her being is stressed in both the effects that she
has on the poet and the innocent nature of the occasions in
which they share. The tremors that begin with their first meeting and extend beyond the limits of *The Vita Nuova* into the
poet's vision of Purgatory (XXX.46–48) lose their religious im-
port if one assumes them to be responses to a wholly fictive personage. If the tremors are self-delusive, so, too, is the poet's
religious awareness, and one must assume that underlying the
delusion there is an extreme subjectivism that belies the work's
rational appeal. One has, in addition, the poet's writings as evidence of a pivotal experience that divides the conventional early
poems from the *dolce stil nova* and *Commedia*. A vocational commitment occurs about the time that scholars assign to the writing of *The Vita Nuova,* and just as one may propose that the
longing for Paradise in the *Commedia* is psychologically a sublimated desire by the exiled poet to return to Florence, one may
make a comparable case for his joining Beatrice in Heaven. This
union compensates for an inability to win her earthly part-
nership. Dante would not be unique in his transforming
unrequited love into a fictive union. Nor is unrequited love an-
tipathetic to vocational or renewed moral commitments. Failure
frequently challenges identity, and melancholy and deepening
self-reflection result. Often the bases of the commitments are already present, and the challenges simply secure their recogni-

tion. Nonetheless, plausibility is not itself absolute guarantee of veracity or sufficient reason on which to conclude that poetic license in a work has been suspended.

The care with which Dante makes certain that "la gloriosa donna della mia mente" appears in situations that in no way embarrass her strengthens the argument of Beatrice's factual existence by implying that a real person might be embarrassed. Their encounters as children are left unexplored since, as Dante says, "to dwell on the feelings and actions of such early years might appear to some to be fictitious." Their adult encounters occur in public and, except for the suggestion that she accepts the poems that the poet writes in her praise, there is little in any of these encounters to encourage the poet's advances. These advances, moreover, are so ambiguous that, even when he is instructed by Love to make his verses "a kind of intermediary," he is reminded that "it is not fitting to address her directly" (XII). They meet on the street (II, III, X) and at a wedding feast (XIV), and in Chapter V, he silently admires her in church. This care along with the clearly defined, discrete social worlds in which the lovers move might easily have become inconsistent or dissolved if *The Vita Nuova* were entirely imaginative. Why has the poet not, for example, allowed the lady to say more than greetings? Or even to give some overt acknowledgment of the poems written in her praise? These actions could be innocent enough, except that they probably never occurred and to suggest they had might harm the book's testimonial nature or be offensive to a real individual. The lack of rhetorical antithesis involving either the early romantic screens or the "donna gentile" of the later chapters argues as well for Beatrice's historical origin.

Passion occurs in episodes that the poet carefully identifies as dream (III, XII), delirium (XXIII), and fantasy or imagination (IX, XXIV, XXXIX, and XLII). Passionate encounter occurs in an effort by him to understand responses like the tremors that are part of the meetings with Beatrice, and it is a function of these subjective interludes to mediate between "the obscure" and "the plain" by imagination if not reason. In *The Convivio,* Dante recognizes the ways in which the eye and the imagination both falsify (IV.xv.168–83), but he also acknowledges that the imagination is an organic virtue which draws to itself what it perceives and that intellect is dependent upon the imagination's accurate apprehension for interpretation (III.iv.72–112). Again, if he had not intended certain parts of *The Vita Nuova* to be factual, he would not have needed to make within the work the boundaries of these subjective states so precise or to say, as he does at the end of Chapter III, that the "true meaning" of his first dream "was not then perceived by anyone, but now it is perfectly clear to the simplest reader." The "clarity" which comes with his overt perception of Beatrice as Christlike in Chapter XXIV, when the knowledge of the prose narrator coincides with that of the poet, is then applied retrospectively to the poems that he had written earlier. Nor does this structural shift between subjective and factual states contradict those critics who feel that the narrative of the work was invented to provide a frame for "selected early poems," since the construction of such a framework in no way affects the factual or nonfactual origin of Beatrice.

But perhaps most importantly, the movement of the book from sensitive to intellectual memory requires a factual beginning, however much the facts may later be transmogrified by intellect. The need is so integral that in the first four centuries of Dante criticism only one commentator questioned the physical reality of Beatrice. As early as *Vita di Dante* (1354–55), Boccaccio is identifying "la gloriosa donna" with Beatrice dei Portinari, the daughter of a prominent Florentine, Folco dei Portinari. By 1288, she was already married to the banker Simone dei Bardi. Boccaccio makes the identification more explicit in his lectures on the *Commedia* (1373–75), and his identification is repeated by the poet's son, Pietro di Dante, in his commentary on *Inferno* II.70. Thus, within fifty years of the poet's death and at a time when the Portinari and Bardi families were still in Florence, they were publicly being implicated in Dante's life. Given the high esteem in which the *Commedia* was already held, the implication might undoubtedly be thought an honor and the identification made for reasons of courtesy and patronage as well as to dignify rumor. Yet, nothing that scholars have been able to document of Beatrice dei Portinari's life contradicts the portrait in *The Vita Nuova*. In the most important of the early commentaries on the *Commedia*, Benvenuto da Imola does not mention a family name, although he is emphatic about the reality of Beatrice. Concerned more with the artistic than the historical nature of the work, only recent scholars have questioned or have dismissed the matters of who Beatrice was and whether she ever existed.

Medieval poetics supports the older, historical approach. As early as *The Confessions,* Augustine "saw visible beauty as only a feeble likeness of the invisible, . . . borne in the soul of the master artist who [was] a kind of mediator between God and the material world." The artist worked "if not from an Idea in the real, metaphysical sense, at least from an inner notion of form, or 'quasi-idea,' that preceded the work." The "quasi-idea" was not notably different from the subjective impulse that "knew" God (IV. I), and in making "quasi-ideas" visible, the artist could not separate the beautiful from the good. Just as God had in Creation, the artist must seek "definite ends through definite means, realizing definite forms in definite materials." Imitations of nature were, consequently, not so much simple mirrorings as participations in the process by which nature creates. Since this process is controlled by a definite teleology, nature is always open to reshaping that will emphasize Christian ends and allow, thereby, the adoration of the "one supreme Beauty that is 'above the souls.' " Art fills in the gap between worldly and Divine fact. Dismissed as a kind of blasphemy was one's allowing an objective impulse like nature undue importance, since it presumed an object divorced from a subject and by extension it might suggest extradivine models guiding God's creative activity. Equally unacceptable was art that suggested a teleology different from that approved by the Church.[2]

Aristotle's view that probable actions were preferable to improbable truths was thus challenged, since the Aristotelian view implied a set system whose axioms might challenge God's. This was especially true of notions like "poetic justice" that gave literature its advantage over history and life by altering Divine judgments in order to serve art's "higher truths." Writers were

---

[2] Erwin Panofsky, *Idea,* tr. Joseph Peake (Columbia: Univ. of South Carolina Press, 1968), pp. 35–43. For a more extended view of medieval poetics as it relates to the lyric, see my *Transformations in the Renaissance English Lyric* (Ithaca, N.Y.: Cornell Univ. Press, 1970), pp. 1–36.

encouraged, rather, to accept the improbable, the "mirabile." Through a process of rationalization poets were expected to bring the "facts" of experience into harmony with what they knew of God's intention. They were encouraged, thereby, to accept life and the historical as the bases on which to create, leaving the assimilation of what they saw to the processes of sympathy and allegorization. On the premise of sympathetic vibrations such forms as the lyric or melic were valued. Music set up in man's soul a microcosmic-macrocosmic relationship to Truth that allowed song to be a reflection on earth of God's arithmetic in heaven. Forms like the epic and narrative whose set systems encourage the illusions of "false worlds" could be brought into "truth" by interpretation. In Galatians (iv.22–26) and 1 Corinthians (iv.9), Saint Paul had allowed for such procedures in regard to Scripture, and in the sixth century, Fulgentius' *Virgiliana continentia* provided a basis for Christian assimilation of pagan literature by interpreting the *Aeneid* as a metaphor of life and the travels of Aeneas as the progress of the human soul from nature, through wisdom, to final happiness. A comparable assimilation occurred in art as the saints depicted in medieval illuminations assumed typical theatrical poses against backgrounds that were derived ultimately from stage sets.

The preponderance of "wonder" and "chance" in *The Vita Nuova* enforces the sense that Dante is adhering to the historical bent of medieval poetics, although a modern reader, conditioned by Aristotle and the *alter deus* of Renaissance poetics, is likely to view the improbabilities of the narrative as evidence of fiction. A recurrence of the number nine is established in the early meetings of the couple and in the hour of Dante's two dreams, Beatrice being ninth in his list of "the sixty most beautiful women in the city," while the discourse on nine which follows her death and occupies the whole of Chapter XXIX emphasizes the importance of the rational process in adjusting the "chaos" of contemporary experience to Divine intent. While the uses of "nine" suggest that some tampering may have been done with fact, they in no way undermine the reality of fact conceived as ciphers in some heavenly encyclopedia. Indeed, one might argue that the rationalizing process of numerology strengthens physical reality by providing it with a transtextuality needed for fact. The existence of the same event in two different schemes tends to make it, first, independent of either scheme and, second, more "truthful," by enlarging through recurrence the area of its verifiability. This argument would also be applicable to the Christ-imagery that surrounds the subjective appearances of Beatrice. An alteration of reality to suit the Truth of Christian history does not make that reality any less factual, since for Christians many life experiences are not seen in their true light and at Judgment Day some modification must occur in order that "sorrow and mourning will flee away" (Revelation xx.12).

Nor do these arguments of fact and historical approach diminish Beatrice's symbolic value. Beatrice is by name ("she who blesses") and essence sacramental. She is a visible sign of an inward grace, initiated by God and subject to the same sign-mystery of Christ's Incarnation. She is, as Dante implies in his Christ-imagery and the discourse on nine, "the historically authentic and actual presence of the eschatologically triumphant mercy of God." Consequently, she is both factual and symbolic in a way that is consistent with the multiple reality of medieval life and foreign to most modern thinking. Her "sacramentality," which explains her effects on Dante, may explain as well part of his much debated reluctance to deal with her death in Chapter XXVIII. How does one deal with the removal of a visible sign without suggesting either the death of the sacrament or the inappropriateness of the metaphor? Grace certainly has not been withdrawn, and altering her sacramental character at this point defeats the apocalyptic vision that she presumably instills. Dante wisely decides that "no words of mine would be adequate to treat the subject as it should be treated," for to treat the subject inadequately might, in fact, push the book beyond the subject announced in the preface or oblige him to write in praise of himself by suggesting, after having indicated her beneficial effects on others, that her sacramental purpose was solely focused on him. Indeed, one suspects that Beatrice's factual value is necessary to her symbolic nature and that the second cannot exist without the first.

This sacramental nature is important not only for *The Vita Nuova* but also for what it tells readers of the nature of the autobiographical poems that directly follow Dante's work. The fact of Beatrice, for instance, encourages readers to accept the fact of the young poet, both as he is described in *The Vita Nuova* and as he comes through as its author. Beatrice, becomes *the* moment in time from which a crucial, if narrow portion of his life comes to be reviewed along historical lines. Decisions which he makes have their consequences in immediate effects so that, in keeping with what W. H. Auden calls "Christian character," the emergent poet writes the history of the effects of possibility.

J. E. Shaw discovers three areas of emergence: the unenlightened author of the early poems; the author of the prose commentaries and the later poems; and finally, the author / scribe copyist of the "little book of memory." All these areas interlace to form a sustained persona that, by the inclusion of early poems, "startlingly bears witness to a change of focus." [3] Topical digressions also occur in Chapters XI, XXV, and XXIX, adding to these changes, but the work as a whole adumbrates a prototype of the "I" of subsequent poetic autobiography. By being sustained and historical, this "I" differs from the lyrical "I" of poets like Sappho who, by defining themselves against established norms and types, achieve individuality but not historical continuity. Similarly, by abandoning the anonymity of the medieval lyric to argue from particulars in the prose segments, Dante affirms an individual moral choice that looks forward to the complex individualisms of the Renaissance.

Beatrice's symbolic nature functions simultaneously to support this factual progress with a spiritual one. Existing outside of time, she combines with Dante / Everyman to form a microcosm of the paradigmatic spiritual history of man's redemption from sin. For Christians, this history begins with a fall from Grace rather than from Heaven, and any time after the removal of Original Sin, a soul can be reborn, as Dante's is, through Grace. Consequently, just as Dante's actions may be viewed on

---

[3] See particularly W. H. Auden, "The Christian Tragic Hero," *New York Times Book Review*, December 19, 1945, pp. 1+, and "The Dyer's Hand," *The Listener*, 53 (1955), 1064; J. E. Shaw, *Essays on The Vita Nuova* (Princeton: Princeton Univ. Press, 1929), pp. 79–82. The phrase, "startlingly bears witness to a change of focus," is taken from Roy Pascal's discussion of diary extracts in autobiography, *Design and Truth in Autobiography* (London: Routledge & Kegan Paul, 1960), p. 5.

a personal level as having to do with character, they may be seen on a spiritual level as relating to a vision of Christian history. Barbara Nowlan's identification of Dante's scribe as "more closely related to the image of John the Evangelist as scribe of the Apocalypse than to images of ordinary monkish scribes" [4] is here useful, for *The Vita Nuova* is an effort to show history from a point of view outside of time. That this point of view should cause the poet trouble in his attempts to end the work is also understandable. *The Convivio* suggests that at one time he may have let the "donna gentile" prevail over his love for Beatrice (II.ii.9), and on the basis of that suggestion, a number of critics have proposed that the version of *The Vita Nuova* that has come down is a later one. This proposal is supported but not proved by an abrupt shift that occurs between the highly emotional conclusion to Chapter xxxix and the sad but almost serene description of the pilgrims traveling to Rome on which the next chapter opens. The shift continues in the concerns of the final sonnet and the equally abrupt decisions "to write no more of this blessed one until I could do so more worthily" and to end with her beholding God "face to face."

These factual and symbolic aspects of Beatrice have their counterparts in the outer and inner worlds that Roy Pascal finds necessary for "good" autobiography. In *Design and Truth in Autobiography,* he keeps the historical separate from the aesthetic process, describing how selection, lapses in memory, and emphasis tend to blur accuracy into significance. For him, significance is primarily vocational: "With religious autobiographers the truth may mean the truth of belief, other writers may

[4] Barbara Nowlan, *"The Vita Nuova:* Dante's Book of Revelation," *Dante Studies,* No. 88 (Albany: Dante Society of America, 1970), p. 76.

choose as their purpose the truth of some outlook or some professional achievement." Angus Fletcher's *The Prophetic Moment*
sees the narrowing of these demonic (historical) and apocalyptic
(aesthetic) drives as productive of a more significant "critical
juncture when the prophetic order of history is revealed." Interested not so much in vocational justification as in the energies
that are generated by literary works that mediate between established genres, he finds prophecy one outcome of mixing high
mimetic and romantic modes. The "analogy to nature and experience" that characterizes high mimetic art reaches a point when
the "analogy of innocence" is again made possible by the opening up of a new level of unprobed reality. Fletcher contends that
the various discoveries of the Renaissance, including those of
classical literature and the New World, made prophecy possible
in works like *The Faerie Queene,* but the possibility is already
part of primitive purification rites and Christian sacrament and
seems to be part, too, of the impulse toward ratiocination in
which autobiographical utterance including *The Vita Nuova* participates.[5]

In autobiography, the participation is usually implicit in a
writer's decision to write of himself. Regardless of whether he
chooses to view his life as celebratory (sharing experience with
others), confessional (unburdening guilt), apologetic (defending

[5] Pascal, p. 61. Angus Fletcher, *The Prophetic Moment* (Chicago: Univ. of
Chicago Press, 1971), p. 45. See also Northrop Frye, *The Anatomy of Criticism*
(Princeton: Princeton Univ. Press, 1957), pp. 141–58, for the terminology of
apocalyptic, demonic, romantic, and high mimetic. I am deliberately shifting
terms in this and the following paragraphs because I believe each of these
writers is coming at the same experience from a different route.

an action or course), or exploratory (revealing hidden motives or meaning), he turns his past into an illustration of something. By abstraction he purifies himself of the nausea of experience. He separates himself both from an earlier being and from the ordinary experiences of his neighbors much as George Herbert Mead indicates is true of anyone who would go "against the whole world about him": "To do that he has to speak with the voice of reason to himself. He has to comprehend the voices of the past and of the future. That is the only way in which the self can get a voice which is more than the voice of the community." He enters what Victor Turner calls a "liminal" state, a "symbolic domain that has few or none of the attributes of his past or coming state" and which is characterized by an equality and comradeship with other "initiands." He approaches a "double character" preparatory to self-consciousness. This state of liminality or "moment in and out of time" may, in addition, permit him to obtain "an approximation, however limited, to a global view of man's place in the cosmos and his relations with other classes of visible and invisible entities." The "domain" frequently comprises the "place" of the autobiographer as he mediates between his past (*Umwelt* and *Mitwelt*) and what he seeks to become (*Eigenwelt*) and, in societies that do not provide adequate or sufficiently frequent formal manifestations, the liminality seems to be expressed as an individual responsibility.[6]

[6] George Herbert Mead, *Mind, Self & Society* (Chicago: Phoenix Books, 1962), p. 168. Victor Turner, *Dramas, Fields, and Metaphors* (Ithaca, N.Y.: Cornell Univ. Press, 1974), pp. 232, 238–40. The term "nausea" is indebted to the writings of Jean-Paul Sartre and "Umwelt," "Mitwelt," and "Eigenwelt" to those of Martin Heidegger.

In *The Vita Nuova,* the apocalyptic and demonic drives are given recognition as the work's pattern of subjective and narrative segments. Prophetic vision occurs either within a subjective interlude or in the poem immediately following. One exception to this pattern is the "imaginazione" of Chapter IX, wherein Love returns the poet's heart and bids him give it to another. Although the poet's inconstancy will precipitate Beatrice's cut in the next chapter, most critics are willing to assign the appearance of Love to a lesser kind of passion than that which exists in the other interludes. A second exception occurs with the prophetic poem of Chapter XLI. The poem follows no immediate subjective interlude. Rather, it precedes the "visione" of the book's final chapter. Nonetheless, the intent of the pattern is established as early as the second chapter when the first meeting of the two inaugurates the tremors that signal the poet's awakening to a higher reality. The greeting of Chapter III furthers this intent, and the narrative follows the implications of the awakening through the early romantic "screens," the cessation of these screens after Beatrice's cut, and the crucial transfiguration of Chapter XIV, which, by its semblance to death and heavenly glory, secures the poet's permanent constancy. This constancy lasts him through subsequent sonnets of praise, shared sorrow at the death of her father, her own death, and finally, after seeking solace with a "donna gentile," to a reconciliation with her heavenly being. Awakenings, lapses, tests, and constancy identify Beatrice as "human desire," and to the extent that Dante is drawn to her, his own impulses are apocalyptic and innocent. To the extent that he is undirected or tempted, his impulses are demonic, natural, and experiential.

A reader's recognition of the communities to which Dante is

led by these impulses depends upon the particular level on which he wishes to interpret the work, although a vague liminality characterizes all its recognitions. Working downward, the highest and most desired community is that of the saved and involves Dante and Beatrice as Everyman and Grace in their most symbolic forms. The next highest and desired community is that of great poets, involving Dante and Beatrice as poet and poetic inspiration in the first of their historical roles. Lesser in desirability is the conventional world of lovers which not only extends the significance of Beatrice to other women but also creates a conflict in Dante between rational and physical desire. All these higher communities work on Dante and Beatrice as they are and indicate that, much as the growth of autobiography can be seen as a response to a loss of traditional liminal structures that social changes foster, the writing of *The Vita Nuova* may well owe something to the poet's decision not to follow his father's vocation but to take advantage of other opportunities that contemporary Florence offered. Like the later Humanists, Dante may have been forced into an individual liminality by the very newness of these opportunities. In a corollary way, the work's positing of a sacrament outside Church control may have been prompted by political insecurity: the existence in the divided city of threats to withdraw the sacraments for political purposes or by the conditions of simony that the poet attacks in the *Commedia*.

In contrast to later autobiographies which tend to present their subjects as accessible behavioral options, Dante's "encounters" with Beatrice leave the reader with no comparable access. The sacramental nature of Dante's experience is unique and, having discovered in a love object a correlative to his innermost

identity, he converts the highly interested focus of current love
poetry to personally disinterested ends. His awareness of the
possibility of such a conversion is implied in Love's articulation
of his nature as resembling center and circumference (XII),
Love's likening of Beatrice's nature to his own (XXIV), and the
subsequent discussion of essence / accident of which rhetorical
personification is one reflection (XXV). The success of the conversion is signalled in the growing demands for the poet's work
that occur in Chapters XXXIII, XXXIV, and XLI, and this success
is again given emphasis in *Inferno* and *Purgatory* in the encounters with great pagan poets (IV.100–102) and later with
Bonagiunta (XXIV.49–57) and Beatrice (XXXI.34–36). Both the
possibility and realization affirm the prophetic renewal of the
work's subjective / objective juncture. This renewal explains
why, after having undergone so many learning experiences,
Dante in the final chapter can still claim "innocence" in his
need to "apply myself as much as I can" before composing "con-
cerning her what has never been written in rhyme of any
woman." Thus, much as Augustine had in *The Confessions,*
Dante presents himself in *The Vita Nuova* as a fellow sufferer
becoming nascent Type. Avoiding the mystic's withdrawal to
Perfection, he is the "revealed" model poet of Christian love,
tied to history by the fact of Beatrice and challenging subsequent poets to follow in his way. He thus extends medieval
typology to contemporary life and literature much as in his
writings he works with non- and post-biblical thought to en-
large biblical cosmology.[7]

---

[7] In *Advent at the Gates* (Bloomington: Indiana Univ. Press, 1974), Mark
Musa offers a provocative interpretation of the Bonagiunta episode and Dante's
singularity, pp. 111–28. For a discussion of Eusebius as a forerunner of Chris-

II

It is to this "typal" Dante and the historical and factual Beatrice that Petrarch turns in deciding to construct his *Canzonieri* about images of Laura. His preference of *The Vita Nuova* to the more symbolic *Commedia* is expressed in a letter (*Fam.* XXX.15), as is his denial of Giacomo Colonna's assertion that he was not in love with a real woman but was personifying his ambitions in a fiction he then called "Laura" (*Fam.* II.9). In the *Secretum,* Petrarch has Saint Augustine reverse Colonna's assertion by claiming that Laura's name created the ambitions Petrarch later assumed. But Petrarch seems to have found the factual Beatrice already too limited in focus to serve as his model.

Rather than a hieratic coalescing of four levels of perception that accords with a polysemous view of reality, Petrarch's Laura multiplies into four different people: a Laura who is his virtuous guide to salvation; a Laura who comes to stand for worldly ambition; a Laura who arouses his sexual nature; and a factual Laura who occasions poems. Petrarch is moved, moreover, by Laura's golden hair and physical appearance instead of by sympathetic vibration. If one accepts Jean Starobinski's notion that a concept of deity functions within autobiography to enforce the autobiographer's truthfulness, thus unifying the form's diverse ranges of experience,[8] one can discern in the parallel images of

---

tian syntheses of history, see A. D. Momigliano, "Pagan and Christian Historiography in the Fourth Century A.D.," in *The Conflict between Paganism and Christianity in the Fourth Century,* ed. A. D. Momigliano (Oxford: Oxford Univ. Press, 1963).

[8] Jean Starobinski, "The Style of Autobiography," in *Literary Style: A Symposium,* ed. Seymour Chatman (New York: Oxford Univ. Press, 1971), p. 286. Starobinski is discussing Jean-Jacques Rousseau's *Confessions,* but the concept

Laura the effects of an expanding universe and the beginnings of the "lateral fall" that will figure prominently in the later visions of Edmund Spenser and John Milton. One travels in and out rather than up and down much as in painting the illusion of depth begins to succeed vertical composition.

The "god" of Petrarch's *Canzonieri* is clearly the *alter deus* of Renaissance poetics. Unlike *The Vita Nuova,* Petrarch's work is arranged by a complex system of chronology, theme, and sense of variety rather than constructed to accord with Divine or historical time. Petrarchan "time," so to speak, is poetic time and subject to the logic of art. The sacramental nature of Beatrice gives way to the sacramental character of the poet's memory, and rather than appear in Beatrice's paradigmatic present tense, Laura appears ever in a past tense that is renewed by the poet's present state. This quality of nostalgia has prompted critics like Thomas Bergin to suggest that "frustration is the poet's constant condition" and "that Petrarch is what we would call nowadays a displaced person." But the condition is part of any art that seeks to define fact by setting up an apposite system with axioms of decorum and justice that preclude coalescing. One moves from the "liminal" conditions of Dante to "outsiderhood," the condition of being "set outside the structural arrangements of a given social system" by either ascription, situation, temperament, or will. Petrarch is compelled to make art his home. Bergin goes so far as to propose that Petrarch's "language is also that of a displaced person, one who speaks his na-

---

goes back to Augustine's assertion, "I speak in your presence, O Lord, and therefore I shall say what is true." See Fletcher, pp. 45–47n, for an extended discussion of "lateral fall" in the English Renaissance.

tive tongue correctly and carefully but not quite colloquially." [9]
Certainly, there is an increase in both plasticity and aural den-
sity at the same time that the instructional character one associ-
ates with liminal states diminishes. Even in death, Laura does
not instruct the poet on matters of theology or celestial topography. She merely waits. The reality that theology and the person
of Beatrice once offered Dante becomes mired in verisimilitude.

With the *Canzonieri,* one can begin to speak realistically of
"fact" and "fiction" as separate entities in poetic autobiography.
Syllogistically, "fact" assumes the status of "conclusion": it is,
as in history, an end, something to which a major premise (historical overview) and a minor premise (personal approach) give
significance, and which, in turn, supports the reality of both
premises. In the *Canzonieri,* as in subsequent art, "fact" becomes
a minor premise, an instance qualifying a major premise and
leading to a "fictional" possibility. Medieval poetics had allowed
the two visions to dissolve into one by making art and the natural process subservient to common axioms, although, as in *The
Vita Nuova,* a second syllogism was often needed to uncover
their commonality. The horizons offered to the Renaissance
mind, however, required that it give imagination and imaginative play priority and make art's relationship to history revolutionary. The difference between the visions became the difference between "what should be" and "what is." Art offered
models toward which the historical mind strove. In poetic autobiography, despite a persistence of intractable reality in events

---

[9] Thomas G. Bergin, *Petrarch* (New York: Twayne Publishers, 1970), pp.
161, 170. Bergin expresses confusion in his trying to account for a rationale in
Petrarch's clusters.

like Laura's death and the poet's aging, these models came to be represented not as something established but as process. A lateral worldly transformation effecting religious reformation came to replace transfiguration just as four representations of Laura replaced a fourfold Beatrice. The change is most apparent in thematic clusters which in the *Canzonieri* approximate the subjective interludes of *The Vita Nuova*. Again, irregularity suggests a "chance universe" and the factual "wonders" on which intellect will build. However, the compressed nature of their conflicting order is rhetorical rather than visionary and ends in parody rather than as an extension of the prophetic mode. One has an imaginative recreation of life whose repetitiousness the Middle Ages might find deterministic but on whose cyclicism Renaissance historiography and subsequent autobiography depend.[10]

Neal Ward Gilbert touches on aspects of this growing literary preference for repetition in his *Renaissance Concepts of Method*. In contrast to prophetic "renewal" where order is integral to perception, order in "methodical" works is integral to the perceiving. It implies that the kind of ongoing growth that allowed Dante to conceive of himself as an extension of biblical type has

---

[10] The fact / fiction dichotomy can be traced back to the gates of horn and ivory in the *Iliad* and to Plato's *Republic*, but by making both elements subservient to Divine intent, medieval poetics colored the way the Renaissance interpreted the division. Often the Renaissance writer shifted from a Platonic concept of visible reality as a repetition of an Ideal Reality to visible reality as a moment in a linear process fulfilling a Divine plan. Repetition looms importantly also in Renaissance concepts of imitation and consistency.

given way to a terminus which permits repetition by recognizing fixed, transferable elements as part of perception. The emphasis is on consistency, uniformity, and efficiency, and the integral values attached to coalescings of center and circumference become submerged in the advantages that imposed, rhetorical predicaments provide. Rules for controlling these predicaments abound. Gilbert points out that in education "the notion that method can provide a short cut to learning an art did not seem crucial to medieval students or educational reformers. Only when the milieu had become more time-conscious did method become the slogan of those who wished to speed up the process of learning. . . . In the words of Girolamo Barro . . . method was the 'brief way under whose guidance we are led as quickly as possible to knowledge.' The insistence on speed is typical of the humanists; the arts must be learned 'as quickly as possible.' " The difficulty that visionary writers have is adjusting their visions to fit these emergent rules which in time become part of a reader's expectations. The adjustments suggest mechanization, and failure to conform to the mechanization accounts for what, in the wake of regulation, critics have termed "transcendental" or "irregular" forms. In *Mimesis,* Erich Auerbach proposes that such "failures" inhere in Christian perception.[11]

---

[11] Neal Ward Gilbert, *Renaissance Concepts of Method* (New York: Columbia Univ. Press, 1960), pp. 66, 71. See also my *Transformations in the Renaissance English Lyric* for discussions of predicaments and the effects of regulation upon the Renaissance lyric, pp. 100–07. Auerbach makes his statement on mixed forms in his discussion of Petronius in *Mimesis,* tr. W. R. Trask (Princeton: Princeton Univ. Press, 1953), pp. 25–49.

III

In the autobiographical and quasi-autobiographical sonnet sequences that pattern themselves on the *Canzonieri,* these tendencies toward repetition and the exclusion of the symbolic functions of Beatrice are even more marked. Continuing the shift from metaphysical to moral concerns, the sequences concentrate on the socializing functions of art and love. If the sequences promise immortality, it is a worldly immortality and not the heavenly goal of Dante's poet. Similarly, if a type is aimed for, it is a type subject to artistic decorum not Truth. Yet by continuing the dynamics of subjective (lyrical) and objective (narrative) elements, the sequences and their descriptions of a world run by Divine rules and divorced from direct Divine intervention reinforce a parody of the prophetic mode. Reacting to one of the most famous of the collections, Sidney's *Astrophel and Stella,* C. S. Lewis notes that "the first thing [readers] have to grasp about the sonnet sequence is that it is not a way of telling a story. It is a form which exists for the sake of prolonged meditation, chiefly on love, but relieved from time to time by excursions into public affairs, literary criticism, compliment, or what you will. . . . [W]hen a poet looks in his heart he finds many things there besides the actual. That is why, and how, he is a poet." But by Sidney's day, the questions that Lewis' reaction raises are already moot. Since the lyric no longer evokes Reality by sympathetic response but persuades one empathetically to action, poets are no longer constricted by historical accuracy in promoting their visions. Autobiographical elements are disguised among attractive fictions which, if anything, prove the sincerity of what is being said by their disguise. Canidia's "sweet portrait," as Sidney remarks, bears only suggestive resemblance to her "who, Horace swears, was foul and ill-favored." [12]

William Wordsworth, coming late in the tradition, labors to get back into poetic autobiography something like Reality and the symbolic nature of Beatrice with the lyrical interludes of *The Prelude*. These moments of "visionary power" occur in nature and culminate in the Mount Snowden episode of the final book. They oppose the "savage torpor" and "benumbing round" of modern life, as the poet reviews their occurrences in an extended narrative of childhood, schooling, poetic consecration, and early debts to literature, and as part of a growing interest in man, involvement with the French Revolution, and a resultant personal despondency. It is from this despondency that the lengthy text of *The Prelude* makes an effort to recover. Critics have commented on the resemblance of Wordsworth's inset lyrical moments to the rhythms of Wordsworth's shorter poems. Carlos Baker, for instance, describes their effect as that of "double exposure": The difference between successive depictions of the same scene signals a growth. M. H. Abrams makes the "double exposure" practice common to Romantic nature lyrics: "The speaker begins with a description of the landscape; an aspect or change of aspect in the landscape evokes a varied but integral process of memory . . . [and] in the course of this meditation

[12] C. S. Lewis, *English Literature in the Sixteenth Century* (Oxford: Oxford Univ. Press, 1954), pp. 327–28; Sir Philip Sidney, "An Apology for Poetry," *Elizabethan Critical Essays,* ed. Gregory Smith (London: Oxford Univ. Press, 1904), I, 201.

the lyric speaker achieves an insight. . . . Often the poem rounds upon itself to end where it began, at the outer scene, but with an altered mood and deepened understanding which is the result of the intervening meditation." The interludes restore "the analogy of innocence" to "the analogy to nature and experience," permitting a prophetic renewal similar to Dante's in Wordsworth's terminal "recognition of transcendent power." As John Morris maintains, the very claim of *The Prelude* that "the act of retrospection and composition is . . . the source of a knowledge higher than the particular truths of the experiences recorded marks Wordsworth's autobiography off from all previous English examples of the form." [13]

More recently *The Cantos* of Ezra Pound deals with the interplay of lyrical and narrative moments along lines derived from the Romantic equation of truth and beauty and a regard for the poet as an "unacknowledged legislator of mankind." Following Matthew Arnold's prediction that in the "failure" of religion and philosophy, "more and more . . . mankind will have to turn to poetry to interpret life," Pound stresses language as the vehicle of the interpretation. For Pound, it is the duty of "the despised litterati" to care for the solidity and validity of words. This care extends to social justice as well as permanent products like art, science, and literature. Great literature be-

---

[13] Carlos Baker, "Introduction," *William Wordsworth's The Prelude* (New York: Holt, Rinehart and Winston, 1954), pp. xvi–xvii; M. H. Abrams, "Structure and Style in the Romantic Nature Lyric," in *From Sensibility to Romanticism,* ed. Frederick W. Hilles and Harold Bloom (New York: Oxford Univ. Press, 1965), pp. 527–28; John N. Morris, *Versions of the Self* (New York: Basic Books, 1966), p. 16.

comes "simply language charged with meaning to the utmost possible degree" and a discovery rather than artifact of the poet. Its origin is not human but divine. In this regard, the most significant "plot" of the work consists in the return of these "eternal states of mind" at increasingly frequent intervals as the poet, like Dante and Petrarch before him, purges himself of more and more of the ugliness of life. This purging increases the book's "analogy of innocence" until what results in the final cantos is not a prophetic order of history but a mystical vision predicated upon aesthetics and intolerant of worldly experience. The poet, thus, becomes John the Evangelist preaching a Book of Aesthetic Revelation and, as such, a demonic parody rather than a fulfillment of biblical type. "Innocence" is the experience that he offers with his proliferation of "eternalities," which come increasingly to resemble the fragments of cubist art.

Yet, however contributory to subsequent poetic autobiographies the subjective / objective elements of *The Vita Nuova* are, the reader striving to understand the nature of Beatrice and the validity that Dante seeks in the work best begins by resisting the separations of fact and fiction that typify these later works. Although anticipating these forms, Dante's work differs from their narratives, which follow to maturity an author's efforts, expectations, desires, struggles, and aspirations. Rather, it is a testimony of man's likeness to God and God's mercy toward man. Choice, as it occurs in *The Vita Nuova,* is absolute choice between good and evil, and occasionally, as in Augustine's *Confessions,* self-preoccupation results. But this self-preoccupation is rooted by its testimonial nature in God's ongoing purpose and Truth. In these matters, even the distortions of memory participate and, in autobiography's subsequent "inward growth or unfolding" and "outward experience" these distortions become parodies of Inner and Outer Truth. Something like the original metaphysical power remains, but the power is inevitably secularly tuned. In *The Anatomy of Criticism*, Northrop Frye rightly reminds the reader of the advantages that have resulted from this conversion of the spiritually existential to the hypothetical. The "turning of the literal act into play" has been "a fundamental form of the liberalizing of life," [14] and one should not underestimate what the transformation has done to increase a sense of variety and to encourage more democratic forms of government. Great ages of revolution are great ages of personal liminality and autobiography. Dante belongs to an age of settled hierarchy, and for his vision of world order, one starts as he does, by acknowledging not "what should be" but Divine and worldly fact.

[14] Frye, p. 148.

DAVID HACKETT FISCHER

❦

The Braided Narrative: Substance and Form in Social History

Historians today are apt to show signs of impatience when asked if their discipline is an art or a science. It is not the banality of the question which bothers them, but the form in which the question is put. Many historians of my acquaintance deeply believe, as an act of faith, that history is *both* an art and a science. They would have it no other way, for it is the duality of the subject which draws them to it. To a working historian the important question is not to know which element to choose, but how to combine them both in a single act. The central problem of historical writing is to create a set of structural and stylistic devices which mediates successfully between the difficult requirements of history-as-science and history-as-art.

Four historiographical generations ago, the problem was solved in a way which brought general satisfaction. But today it is open again, and its solution is obscure. To understand what has happened, we must understand how the writing of history has changed. In a word, there has been a Revolution—a thought-revolution very much like those which are described in Thomas Kuhn's major essays on the history of science and in Michel Foucault's studies of social thought.[1] Four generations

[1] Thomas Kuhn, *The Structure of Scientific Revolutions* (Chicago: University of Chicago Press, 2nd ed., 1970).

ago, there was a paradigm or *episteme* of historical knowledge which was generally recognized and widely accepted. A writer had only to call his book a history in order to tell his reader what sort of book it was, for history books were very much the same. History was always about the past. It was a narrative craft—a story-telling discipline. And its stories were about the institutionalization of power and authority. All historians were not political historians, but most historians were interested in the politics of whatever subjects they studied. Labor historians were interested in labor leaders; historians of education were concerned with educational organizations and the people who ran them. There were large masses of lesser folk who came and went through the history books, or loitered in the wings like anonymous armies of extras on a Hippodrome stage. But the leading actors were always a small and highly individuated power elite.

Historians tended to study these figures through documentary sources. The results of their study were organized in narrative form and delivered as personal testimony, sometimes with specific citations, but for the most part, historians said to their readers, "I have steeped myself in the sources, and here is what I believe to have happened," and they *were* believed, for this was a time when scholars were gentlemen, and a gentleman was as good as his word.

All of this activity produced a single coherent and plausible conception of history, a paradigm which was at once an idea of the past and a way of knowing it. However often historians disagreed—in fact, even in their disagreements—history itself was a unified discipline, a synthesis of structured thought. Its masters were the great "narrative" historians, of whom the first (in every sense) was Gibbon, followed by Macaulay, Michelet, Ranke, Parkman, and Henry Adams.

This paradigm of history still exists in the world. But it cannot be said to be flourishing. The youngest of its masters is Samuel Eliot Morison, who is now nearly ninety years old. There are no younger narrative historians of comparable ability anywhere in sight.[2]

In the early years of this century, the paradigm of "narrative history" began to come apart. Suddenly there were many interests and questions which did not fit within it. Anomalies of many kinds were found. Young historians were promoted primarily for finding them. For two generations—the generations which flourished from the first decade of the twentieth century to the 1960's—historians became hunters of the great anomalous fact. Each of their successes (and there were many) was a blow against the structure of the old synthesis, which was soon reduced to a ruin. There were some scholars who kept it alive in a private world, and others who labored to restore it. A few heroically attempted to create a new synthesis—in American

---

[2] One of the last great American works of this sort was Allan Nevins' *Ordeal of the Union* (New York, 1947–1971), a history of the civil war in eight volumes. The last two volumes were published posthumously in 1971. In a moving tribute to the author, Vann Woodward pronounced a benediction upon a great scholar and a lamentation for a lost genre. "We are not likely to see more history of this character and scope—millions of words of narrative on a single theme—for some time to come. . . . Narrative has increasingly come to be regarded as superficial, an inadequate means of making the past intelligible. It has given way before the analytical urge." *New York Times,* December 26, 1971.

history, scholars such as Turner, Beard, and Parrington in one generation, Richard Hofstadter, and Daniel Boorstin, Louis Hartz in another. Their work could be understood as a series of paradigm-sketches. But none of these tentative suggestions proved very satisfactory to very many scholars for a very long time. Nobody could put the pieces together again. Historians began to do different things—and also to do them *differently.* There was a period (circa 1930–70) when historical relativism came into fashion, and every convention of the American Historical Association became an organized expression of *angst.*

Today, something new is happening in the historical world. There is a generation of historians just coming to maturity who are the architects of a new synthesis of historical scholarship. The teachers of this generation were, most of all, a group of gifted French historians led by Marc Bloch and Lucien Febvre, who in 1929 founded the most important historical publication of the twentieth century—the journal called *Annales.* Today, their progeny, who are multiplying rapidly throughout the western world, are called the *"Annales* school." There were other pioneers in England, America, and Scandinavia, but even now, thirty-five years after the first issue of *Annales* appeared, the French are still our teachers. The new history is growing from a Gallic root.

We are beginning to understand what this new history will be like. It differs from the earlier historical paradigm in many ways. First, and most fundamentally, it isn't really about the past at all, but rather about change—with past and present in a mutual perspective. Second, it isn't a story-telling but a problem-solving discipline. Third, its problems are not primarily about power, but rather they are about major patterns of change and continuity in the ordinary acts and thought of ordinary people—people in the midst of others—people in society.

The new paradigm of history draws upon many forms of evidence—documents, of course, but also statistics and physical artifacts and iconographic materials and survey research and much more. And from these sources, its empirical findings are reported not as testimony but argument, in which premises and logical procedures are explicitly raised to a level of consciousness.

In short, history today is a hard science. Relativism is now known to be an error. *Annales* history (or social history, as I shall call it) has strict rules of evidence and inference and a strong empirical basis. An historian today is expected not merely to make true statements, but also to demonstrate their truthfulness with such precision and detail that any other historians who have a mind to do so may repeat his empirical inquiries and reproduce his results. It is, I think, precisely that principle of replication which makes history a science. This is to dissent from the common opinion that history is unlike the natural sciences in that its experiments cannot be repeated. An historian's experiment is his research. In that respect there is no difference between historical science and natural science.

History is also increasingly a mathematical science, which speaks in numbers and symbols. It uses the language of mathematics not merely for a quantitative purpose, but also as a calculus of conceptual relationships. Mathematics in history is both a measurement-device and a form of logic.

But at the same time that historians are learning to do all

these things, they are also trying to preserve the ancient literary aspirations of their discipline. Even on the extreme methodological left wing of the profession, that lively little group of econometric historians who call themselves "cliometricians" are members of the only metric discipline which requests the services of a muse. Even the most inveterate quantifiers know themselves to be engaged in a literary enterprise.

Of course, anyone who sets pen to paper can be accused of perpetrating a literary act. In that sense, of literature with a small *l,* every empirical discipline is a literary discipline. But historians hope for something more than merely that. They might also be accused of Literature with a large *L,* literature in the first degree, which is willful and premeditated literature. They deliberately seek to create a work which has an aesthetic and an ethical and a metaphysical dimension, at the same time that they try to remain true to the scientific requirements of their calling.

Most historians today still share these literary aspirations. But none has yet succeeded in solving the difficult problems of structure and style which are posed by the new paradigm. Perhaps nobody will do so until the next generation. The Gibbon of the *Annales* school is probably alive today, sitting in *her* highchair somewhere in an American suburb,[3] turning the pages of Genevieve Foster. When that formidable child comes to maturity, social history will become an art form as highly developed as another sort of history had been four generations ago.

[3] The pronoun gender represents something more than an attempt to avoid the fury of my feminine colleagues. It is sustained by the science of statistical probability.

Today the new paradigm is still in a preliminary stage of development. But if the solution has not yet appeared, we may find a few clues to its probable form in recent work. Some very successful history has been written in the past forty years. Let us choose a few exemplary works and study their success. In France there are the classics of the *Annales* school, of which I shall mention four. Marc Bloch's history of feudal society will surely be on everybody's list. And most historians would also join me in adding three great specimens of the *grande thèse:* Fernand Braudel's history of the Mediterranean world in the age of Philip II, Pierre Goubert's social history of the people of Beauvais, and Emmanuel Le Roy Ladurie's study of the peasants of Languedoc. In English history, I would choose two works—Ronald Syme's *Roman Revolution* and Lewis Namier's *Structure of Politics on the Accession of George III.* In America, four works come to mind: Perry Miller's *New England Mind: The Seventeenth Century;* Peter Gay's *The Enlightenment;* Marvin Meyers' *Jacksonian Persuasion;* and John Demos' *Little Commonwealth.* [4]

[4] Marc Bloch, *Feudal Society,* 2 vols. (Chicago: University of Chicago Press, 1964); Fernand Braudel, *The Mediterranean and the Mediterranean World in the Age of Philip II* (New York: Harper & Row, 1972); Emmanuel Le Roy Ladurie, *Les Paysans de Languedoc,* first published with all the Gallic regalia of a *grande thèse* by the famous VIe section of the Ecole Pratique des Hautes Etudes (Paris: S.E.V.P.E.N, 1966). An abridged paperback was published under much the same title by Flammarion in 1969. An English translation is in progress. Pierre Goubert's *grande thèse* is titled *Beauvais et le Beauvaisis de 1600 à 1730* (Paris: S.E.V.P.E.N 1960). An abridged paperback edition is titled *Cent Mille Provinciaux au XVII" siècle* (Paris: Flammarion, 1968). Ronald Syme, *The Roman Revolution* (Oxford: Oxford University Press, 1939); Lewis Namier, *The Structure of Politics at the Accession of George III,* second edition (London: Macmillan, 1961); Perry Miller, *The New England Mind: The Seventeenth Century*

Some of these works belong to our transitional generations, notably those of Syme and Namier, who were still primarily interested in problems of power, and in that sense traditional. But both of these books are social histories of politics and in that sense innovative. Perry Miller's work was deeply flawed by an idealist epistemology which belongs more to the first paradigm. But in its intricate sense of the structure of its subject it belongs to the second paradigm.

We shall consider three questions in turn: First, the problem of structure in social history. Given the fact that a social historian cannot organize his work around a simple story line, how can he put the pieces together? Second, given the fact that a few dramatic political personalities can no longer play a pivotal role in the work, how can a social historian solve the problem of his *personae?* Third, there is the problem of tone or texture. Given the fact that social historians must prove their statements even in the act of making them, how can the apparatus of proof be incorporated gracefully in the work?

Structure in Social History: The Braided Narrative

The most difficult problem which a social historian faces is structural in nature. It is a problem of substance and form, art

---

(Cambridge, Mass.: Harvard University Press, 1954); Peter Gay, *The Enlightenment: An Interpretation* (New York, Knopf, 1969); Marvin Meyers, *The Jacksonian Persuasion: Politics and Belief* (Stanford, Calif.: Stanford University Press, 1957); John Demos, *The Little Commonwealth: Family Life in Plymouth Colony* (New York: Oxford University Press, 1970).

I should like to add works of German scholarship, chief among them perhaps those of Helmut Böhme. But the new way has spread slowly in Germany, partly because the old way was stronger there than elsewhere, partly because of the destruction of free inquiry during the Nazi era.

and science, all at once. Four generations ago the problem scarcely existed, for narrative historians found a simple and effective solution to their most fundamental problems of structure in their central story lines. Within the narrative structure there were of course many nagging problems. But the central problem was solved by a narrative theme.

Social history is much more difficult to write. Our written language is linear. A ribbon of print is extruded on a page. But the truths of social history are for the most part nonlinear. The subject moves on many lines all at the same time. Society is commonly understood today, in the jargon of the social sciences, as a system—complex set of causal regularities. For the suffering writer of systemic social history and for the still more suffering reader, there is hope in its regularity, but despair in its complexity.

Let us examine the structure of our exemplary works. The first thing we notice is that none but Syme's has a single story line of the sort which appeared in Gibbon or Macaulay or Parkman or Henry Adams. The first volume of Perry Miller's *New England Mind,* for example, has *no* narrative in it. It is a study in arrested motion—a snapshot, so to speak, of the Puritan mind, and not a moving picture. Its architecture is of the most perfect palladian symmetry. It is divided into four parts, each with four chapters, none of which tell a story. Each of them is an analysis of an aspect of puritan thought, not as it changed in time but as it existed in a moment of time.

Running through each analytical unit of Perry Miller's monograph there is a common theme, which is built around a conflict within the inner life of Puritanism—a conflict which, if Miller is correct, the Puritans attempted to resolve by their "covenant" or federal theology. The covenant provides a coherence both for the Puritans and for Perry Miller, who builds his entire work around it. The structure of the work is complex. There are many tension lines. And yet all of them pass through the central idea of the covenant which ties the work together. Instead of a narrative, there is an analytic-synthetic structure of quite a different kind.

Is the architecture of Miller's *New England Mind* the classical solution to the problem? I think not. Even for Miller himself, the structure of Volume I was not useful in solving the problem of Volume II, where the subject was set in motion and the palladian symmetry disappeared in a whirl of movement. Sooner or later, every historian must set his subject in motion through time—or place his subject within it. And to do either of those things is necessarily to introduce an element of narration to the work.

Our structural problem could easily be solved, if we could choose either a narrative or an analytic structure. But in the new social history, the structural problem is complicated by a double requirement—narrative *and* analysis.[5] How might they be combined? In some of our exemplary works, we find an answer.

The works of the *Annales* school tend to be held together by a dialectical tension between two things which the *Annalistes* call *"structure"* and *"conjoncture."* The meaning of these words is problematical—even to the people who use them. The house journal of the *Annales* school contains many essays in definition.

[5] A similar thought is better expressed by Peter Gay: "Historical narration with analysis is trivial, historical analysis without narration is incomplete." *Style in History* (New York: Basic Books, 1974), p. 189.

But, in common usage, *conjoncture* means movement, mutation, change. In some works it might be translated as "tendency." In others, as "patterns of change." [6] The term is untranslatable by any single English word. *Conjoncture* is to structure as movement is to stability, as trend is to context, as *le mouvement court* is to *la longue durée.*

If we study Pierre Goubert's monograph on Beuvais, we find that the work moves, after a perfectly ingenious introduction which is a model in itself, through a series of structures: demographic, economic, and social—structures profound and nearly immobile. The second half of the work (much spoiled in the abridged version) is conjunctural—a study of major fluctuations in the economy, population and society. The work as a whole acquires its structure from the intricate interweaving of *structure* and *conjoncture.* Another *Annales* monograph—Le Roi Ladurie's—rests upon the same distinction between structure and conjuncture, but the two elements are introduced simultaneously and not in turn. The result is a tighter synthetic unity, perhaps with a loss in analytic clarity.

[6] One *Annalist* (if I may use that expression) writes, "Sous beaucoup de plumes 'conjoncture' devient un mot savant pour 'mouvement,' et les 'fluctuations de la conjoncture,' un vulgaire pléonasme. L'opposition avec la 'structure,' reputée stable, parvient mal à donner un contenu au concept." Jean Prudhomme, "Un Apport de J. Marcewski à l'étude de la conjoncture." *Annales,* 20 (1965), 337–46. Some French scholars, economists particularly, reserve "conjoncture" for a particular pattern of movement, for business cycles, as opposed to the process of economic growth on the one hand and seasonal variations on the other. An excellent, brief discussion appears in Alisdair MacIntyre, "Causality in History," *Essays on Explanation and Understanding,* Manninen and Tuomela, eds. (Dordrecht-Holland: Reidel, 1976), pp. 137–58.

Let us look at a very different work, Peter Gay's *Enlighten-*
ment. Here we find a dialectical structure, explicitly conceived in
classical Hegelian terms. The first part, called the "Appeal to
Antiquity," and the second, "The Tension with Christianity,"
represent in the author's thought "two essential elements in the
dialectical progression from which the Enlightenment's radical
program developed." [7] The third part, called "The Pursuit of
Modernity," was "the synthesis of that struggle." The Hegelian
dialectic has become a very common form of braided narrative.

Still another form of braided narrative is built upon a paradox, a play of apparent opposites in theme or interpretation;
this model is found in Marvin Meyers' beautifully crafted *Jack-*
sonian Persuasion and in many other monographs. My dictionary
defines a paradox as a "seeming contradiction." Marvin Meyers'
work gains its coherence from a tension of apparent opposites
which the author discovers in his subject, describes, and then
resolves. He asks, who or what a Jacksonian might have been.
And he answers, "a venturous conservative." To identify the
Jacksonian as a person who is at once venturing and conserving
is to set in motion two very different rhythms, two different
temporal structures, in such a way as to allow the author to deal
in a single unified fashion with a complex idea of his subject.

There are many other varieties of braided narrative. One
common version in today's historical literature is a problem
chain. Each problem leads to a solution which becomes a second
problem which leads to a third problem, and so on. And the
solutions are apt to be entwined in a complex narrative struc-

---

[7] Peter Gay, *The Enlightenment,* I, xii.

ture. If a personal example might be allowed, I am trying to organize a general history of American society on this model. The work begins with a question about demographic history. We discover an answer which requires us to ask another question about economic history. And the economic question, in turn, leads us from the production of wealth to its distribution. The distribution of wealth raises a question about the distribution of power. And the differences which we find between the two bring us to a question about the means of their reconciliation, which we discover in changing patterns of association. Association leads to social roles, and social roles to socialization, etc., etc. By this method we study American society as a population system, a wealth system, a stratification system, a power system, an association system, a psychic system, a socialization system, and much more. Each of these systems has a structure of great complexity, which requires analysis. But each structure has a history, which requires narrative. The elements of narrative and analysis are interwoven in a braided narrative.

The tension of a taut story-line is gone, but history remains a narrative discipline. Social historians tend to think of their work as not a story-telling but a problem-solving discipline. But the solutions to their problems commonly take a complex narrative form, in which many story-lines are braided together by dichotomy, dialectic, paradox or problem-chain.

Our first fumbling attempts at this sort of braiding are apt to produce rather lumpy results. But not always. A classical model is Marc Bloch's *Feudal Society,* which is broken into two volumes, each with its own narrative motif. The first volume is about the birth of feudal society; the second is about its development and decline. Within each volume, and also within each narrative theme, there are a series of analytical sections, each of which tells a story. In Volume I alone, I counted sixty-seven narratives, all running simultaneously through time, each with its own periodicity. These stories are joined with such consummate skill that the reader never notices their number. He is conscious only of one story, conscious of complexity but also of unity.

There are many other ways to combine narrative and analysis. When we turn to a graceful little book by John Demos on the family in Plymouth, we find once again that the main body of the work is organized analytically, with virtually no narrative in any of its eleven chapters. Instead, there is an intricate interplay of analytical themes. The first part, with three chapters on the physical environment of the family, is followed by a second, on the structure of the household itself. The two parts together are dialectically joined in the third part which is a normative study of patterns of psychic development through infancy, childhood, and adolescence. None of this appears as a story, and yet all of it is framed by two narrative chapters: an introduction which is a narrative of Plymouth and a conclusion which is a narrative history of the American family. In short, we find, in John Demos's work, still another way of combining narrative and analysis, a way well suited to the requirements of a period study.

These requirements are at once aesthetic and empirical. Often, the structure of an historical work, as well as its substance, is based upon empiricism. The architecture of a work of social history is offered to the reader as a *fact,* a true statement about past events. It is not the only factual statement that might be made about its subject, but it is so designed that its factuality is demonstrable.

The Personae of Social History: Prosopography, the Modal Personality and Representative Men

Another problem for a social historian is that of his personae. This problem was often beautifully resolved within the first paradigm. Many a great story was strung between the poles of two contending personalities, as in Parkman's *Montcalm and Wolfe*. The psychic intensity of the characterizations in Gibbon and Macaulay and Henry Adams were an important structural component of their works. As long as historians were writing about small groups of extraordinary people they had a very great advantage.

But what is a social historian to do? Here is a problem which nobody has successfully solved. Perry Miller and many others tried to solve it by inventing the fiction of a group mind, the New England Mind, which acquired a life and a character of its own. That fiction worked well enough for literary purposes, but failed the scientific tests.

A better solution is something called "prosopography" in the jargon of the trade, which was developed by Syme and Namier into a major school of English historical scholarship.[8] Prosopography is a method of group biographies, not rounded biographies, but sketches of major figures or of ranges of modal, representative figures who do not receive full biographical treatment.

[8] Good discussions of this subject appear in Lawrence Stone, "Prosopography," in *Daedalus,* 100 (Winter 1971), 46–79; and in Arnold Toynbee, *Acquaintances* (New York: Oxford University Press, 1967), pp. 63–85.

They are sketches located at the points of intersection between individual lives and the sociological lines of the inquiry. This device solves the problem of anonymity in the new history. And it fully meets the requirements of science.

A prosopographer understands his social subject as an elaborate network of particular people. He describes the network in terms of their particularity. Prosopography works well when one is studying small groups of people or for groups which one is studying from the perspective of one particular problem; for the people in a prosopographical history, like cells in a honeycomb, are often in contact on only a single edge.

It is also possible to combine prosopography with the *histoire totale* of the *Annales* school when the subject is small community, which is the characteristic American form of *Annales* history. But prosopography has its limits. Any social historian can use it some of the time. But nobody can use it when history is about very large groups of people, or about a group of great obscurity, or a group of great complexity. Then we must find another way to humanize our history.

Another device, which is more versatile than prosopography, is the use of modal characters. A social historian often uses quantitative tools to make what statisticians call a "measure of central tendency." Two common measurements of this sort are widely used today: the mean and the median. But there is also a third measure of central tendency which is not very widely employed, something that statisticians call the mode, which is the number or value which occurs most frequently in any given series.

In the same sense, we may speak of a modal character, a person whose qualities of mind or character, are, within some specific context, representative of a modal tendency. One may use a set or range of modal characters in juxtaposition. A very good example of this technique is Marvin Meyers' use of it in his study of the *Jacksonian Persuasion* in his sketches of Sedgwick, Leggett, or Rantoul.

An entire structure could be built upon a series of modal characters. Or they could be used within another structure. Each modal character could be developed in the new social history with all the psychic power of the characterizations of Gibbon and Macaulay. In early modern history personal documents are so generally abundant that modal characterizations can be reconstructed within every class and occupation. In American history we possess literally thousands of autobiographies of small farmers and their wives, laborers, seamen, servants, and slaves. This vast literature remains largely unexploited by social historians. It provides many possibilities for modal characterization of a sort which will probably provide the most effective solution to the problem of the personae in social history.

Still a third solution to the problem of humanizing a work of social history is that of the representative character, taking representative in Emerson's sense, rather than a statistician's. We find a model in Eric Cochrane's extraordinary history of Florence in the period 1527–1800.[9] Cochrane's book is divided into six sections, each devoted to the history of Florence at a particular point in time: the 1540's, the 1590's, the 1630's, the 1680's, the 1740's and the 1780's. And each section is organized around

[9] Eric Cochrane, *Florence in the Forgotten Centuries, 1527–1800* (Chicago: University of Chicago Press, 1973), vi, 231–307.

a central figure whose life experiences are described in such a way as to encompass the life of the town. Section IV, for example, is centered on an obscure character named Lorenzo Megalotti. The table of contents is as follows:

Through Megalotti's adventures much can be told and more can be suggested about the social history of Florence in the 1680's. The problem of personae and the problem of structure are solved at the same time by this method.

The Texture of Social History:
The Problem of Notes and Numbers.

There is still a third serious structural problem for any historian who is working today. It is a problem of the texture of the work—the problem which is presented by the apparatus of empirical proof—by those hard lumps of historical learning which so often seem indissoluble to the writer and indigestible to the reader.

The new paradigm of history, as I mentioned before, demands not merely that historians must make true statements, but also that they must demonstrate their truthfulness. That requirement is a heavy burden upon any aspiring author. It requires him to communicate with his readers on many levels at once. At the same time that he tries to create a braided narrative in some very intricate pattern which is at once empirically accurate and aesthetically pleasing, and at the same time that he spins his prosopographical web or creates his modal personalities—at the same time, in short, that he tells his readers in all these ways what he has found, he must also tell them how he found it, what his evidence is, where it is located, and how to get there. Worse, it sometimes seems that every major generalization in social history must be surrounded for its own protection by squadrons of substantive "ifs" and "buts," "perhapses" and "possibles," "might-have-beens" "never-minds," and "on-the-other-hands." The more important the historical generalization becomes, the heavier its historiographical escort of qualifiers and disclaimers and finetuners must be.

Four generations ago, the so-called "narrative-historians" were very impatient with all of this impedimenta of historical scholarship—which they tended to keep in their noteboxes and out of their work. As long as historians tended to testify to their truths, they could do so with impunity. But today, when testimony has been replaced by argument, the problem is acute. The epistemic burden of proof has shifted in scholarship. In the old historiographical world, a reputable historian was believed until he was found to be in error. And then he was presumed to be always in error. Today the statements of a reputable historian are not believed until they are shown to be believable: a much healthier basis for professional interaction. But from a stylistic point of view, it is often very awkward.

The only solution to the problem is the footnote. If the historical monograph is to be a major art form, then a social historian must study the aesthetics of the footnote. The lowly footnote is presently a thing of small repute. A good many people with different motives have conspired to damage its reputation. Publishers have their own reasons for despising notes, which are known to drive up costs and are thought to drive down sales. Teachers commonly urge students to keep their notes to a bare minimum. In manuals of historical style a substantive footnote is said to be bad form. Popular historians believe that footnotes tend to destroy the momentum of their simple story lines and to discourage readers.

All of these attitudes are understandable. But they are also erroneous. They rest upon a very low estimate of a reader's powers of intelligence and concentration. And they ignore the success with which the great historians of the past used notes as stylistic devices.

Gibbon made heavy use of footnotes, which were not merely a decorative species of baroque embellishment suitable to both the time and place and to the author's personality. Gibbon's notes are important to the architecture of his work. They are often very long; on many pages, longer than the text. There are sometimes notes upon notes, and they were used in many different ways.

One set of notes was used for purposes of citation, not as an historian today does so, but rather as part of a web of testimony. Gibbon often demonstrated the quality of his intentions by describing the quantity of his materials. In one note he casually cited the entire corpus of Muratori's transcripts. "As that treasure is in my library," he wrote, "I have thought it an amusement, if not a duty, to consult the originals." Now, Muratori's transcripts ran to thirty-eight volumes. At another point he included extracts from a primary source, and added a note, "these original and authentic acts I have translated with freedom and yet fidelity." [10] Any social historian who wrote such a note today would be eaten alive.

Gibbon often (not always) used his citations primarily as anchors for testimony rather than argument. In that respect his example is irrelevant to the work of historians today. And yet, in another way, a social historian could learn from his success. There is one hilarious example in a note on the siege of Bosra in A.D. 633. For stylistic reasons too tedious to explain, it was important to Gibbon that the bells of Bosra should have been set to ringing wildly as the Saracens stormed the town. There was a source which gave Gibbon his stylistic opportunity and he made the most of it. And yet even as Gibbon seized his opportunity, his conscience required him to add a confession that his source was very corrupt. He did so in an unrepentant footnote which asked, "Did the bells actually ring in Bosra?" Were there any bells to be rung in that unhappy town? When were bells introduced to Asia Minor? All these questions were answered in

[10] Gibbon, *Decline and Fall of the Roman Empire,* 3 vols. (Bury ed., New York: The Heritage Press, 1946), III, 2,369, 2,380.

a learned disquisition on the history of bell ringing in the Mediterranean world, drawn from English, Italian, Greek, Roman, and Arabic sources. It is a joy to read. And the curious effect of all this heavy scholarship was actually to lighten the work. The pedantic apparatus of argumentative proof was brilliantly used for both an empirical and an aesthetic purpose.[11]

His citations did not at all diminish the literary power of his work but actually enhanced it. To publish Gibbon without his notes (as often he *is* published today) is to commit an act of literary vandalism. Gibbon used his footnotes in many ways which were integral to his work. He employed some of them as parentheses, within which he compared tendencies in the ancient and modern world. When he did so, he was creating a beautiful specimen of braided narrative such as appears in social history today. He also used notes to add life to his narrative, as in a learned footnote on changes in the color of the crosses which crusaders sewed to their garments.[12] And he used them for much of his moralizing.

Gibbon's substantive footnotes sometimes grew to the proportions of small essays without in any way diminishing the literary stature of the work, but actually enlarging it. A social historian could profit by his example. There are, of course, limits, and proportions to be observed. The constructive model of Gibbon might be balanced by the cautionary model of Bayle, whose Dictionary appeared with footnotes, sidenotes and topnotes. A small patch of text in the center of the page was surrounded by dark clouds of pedantry which filled every margin. A footnote

[11] Gibbon, III, 1,794.
[12] Gibbon, III, 2,029.

should, of course, be done with a light touch; the heavier the apparatus of learning which is required by the argument, the lighter the touch should be.

Also, if I might employ a railroad analogy, a proper footnote is not a spur but a siding, with switches at both ends. Most historians switch out the reader smoothly enough, but forget to switch him in again. The reader runs to the end of the note, and falls off the track. Perry Miller was a master of the substantive footnote—whenever he chose to use it. He knew how to switch the reader out and in again. We might learn from his success, particularly in the revised version of his "Marrow of Puritan Divinity." [13]

As with notes, so also numbers. A similar problem of texture presents itself in statistical form. The incorporation of statistics in a text is one of the most difficult stylistic problems of social history. It has become common practice for people to push off the statistics to the end, a practice of journal editors today and many monographers. A case in point is a recent work on slavery by two self-styled cliometricians. The work appeared in two small volumes; the muse was present in Volume I and the metrics in Volume II. This, I think, won't do. It won't suffice for any given work of history to be an art and a science *seriatim*. The two must be combined in a single expressive act.

Can they be? I think that Gibbon once again suggests the possibility. The problem of integrating statistics within a prose argument is a problem of integrating two different languages.

---

[13] The reader might examine as one specimen example the note about Anne Hutchinson in "Marrow of Puritan Divinity," in *Errand into the Wilderness*, (Cambridge: Harvard University Press, 1956), p. 84.

This is similar to the problem which Gibbon faced in the use of materials in Latin and Greek within an English text. He solved it by setting his classical passages in such a way that a reader has a choice of reading or not reading them. Either way, the work preserves its coherence.

Gibbon's triumph suggests that the problem has a solution. Perhaps most successful in applying it today is Le Roi Ladurie, who made *"un grand cycle agraire"*—that is, a set of statistical tendencies—into "le personage central" of his book.[14] We shall see many similar attempts in the social history of the next few years. It is a rare monograph today which is not festooned with lorenz curves and punctuated with numbers. But if we can establish rhetorical hierarchies of quantitative complexity, if we can integrate the major tendencies in the text and put the proofs in substantive footnotes and appendices, then numbers and charts and diagrams may actually become a source of stylistic strength rather than weakness. Numbers might indeed become a way of "enlarging the historians' vocabulary" [15] and enriching the text by accent and emphasis.

Conclusion

In short, it seems to me that the progress of social history, as both an art and a science, consists in the development of new forms of narration, the use of new techniques of characterization, and the refinement of all the apparatus of scholarship.

[14] Le Roi Ladurie, *Paysans de Languedoc* (Flammarion ed.), p. 345.

[15] Daniel Boorstin, "Enlarging the Historian's Vocabulary," in R. W. Fogel and S. L. Engerman, eds., *The Reinterpretation of American Economic History* (New York: Harper, 1971), pp. xi–xiv.

The braided narrative, the modal characterization, and the essay note, are the most satisfactory solutions to the problems which are presented by the new history.

As these techniques, and others like them, are slowly perfected, social history is entering a new era of formalism, after having happily survived an antiformalist period of great intensity. The "paradigm changes" of history-as-science find their parallels or counterparts in the transformations of history-as-art. And perhaps the art form called social history is moving on parallel lines with other art forms too. I wonder, without really knowing, but only from an historian's faith in the temporal fitness of things, if similar transformations might be observed in contemporary fiction, poetry, drama, criticism, and the plastic arts. But that is a question for others to answer.

EDWARD W. SAID

≈§§≈

On Repetition

Near the end of *The New Science,* after having laid forth in detail
the precise way in which human history is not only made by
men but also made by them according to cycles (*corsi*) that
repeat themselves (*ricorsi*), Vico then proceeds to explain how
these repeating patterns are intelligent patterns that "preserve
the human race upon this earth." The whole section is a kind of
Platonic meditation upon ideal history. Nevertheless the detail
of what Vico describes is not quite Platonic:

> It is true that men have themselves made this world of na-
> tions (and we took this as the first incontestable principle of
> our Science, since we despaired of finding it from the philoso-
> phers and the philologists), but this world without doubt
> issued from a mind often diverse, at times quite contrary, and
> always superior to the particular ends that men had proposed
> to themselves; which narrow ends, made means to serve wider
> ends, it has always employed to preserve the human race
> upon this earth. Men mean to gratify their bestial lust and
> abandon their offspring, and they inaugurate the chastity of
> marriage from which the families arise. The fathers mean to
> exercise without restraint their paternal power over their
> clients, and they subject them to the civil powers from which
> the cities arise. The reigning orders of nobles mean to abuse

their lordly freedom over the plebeians, and they are obliged to submit to the laws which establish popular liberty. The free peoples mean to shake off the yoke of their laws, and they become subject to monarchs. The monarchs mean to strengthen their own positions by debasing their subjects with all the vices of dissoluteness, and they dispose them to endure slavery at the hands of stronger nations. The nations mean to dissolve themselves, and their remnants flee for safety to the wilderness, whence, like the phoenix, they rise again. That which did all this was mind, for men did it with intelligence; it was not fate, for they did it by choice; not chance, for the results of their so acting are perpetually the same.[1]

The gist of this passage is that any examination of the concrete facts of human history, which is accessible neither to a philosopher nor to a philologist, reveals a principle or force of inner discipline within an otherwise disorganized series of events. Men, Vico says, are wilful irrational creatures whose way with other men or women is sadistic, cruel, or fearful. Fathers bully their wives and children; rulers enslave the people; nations are driven by a suicidal urge to dissolve themselves. History seems therefore to be a drift of occurrences generated by arbitrary passions. Yet what men intend to do, which is nearly always wasteful and would lead to a dead end, is always modulated by the persistence of an intelligent, contrary human force, which Viro calls mind. Mind is the general system of brakes that restrain

[1] *The New Science of Giambattista Vico,* trans. Thomas Goddard Bergin and Max Harold Fisch (Ithaca, N.Y.: Cornell Univ. Press, 1968), p. 425.

the always accelerating irrationality of human behavior. Out of each instance of men's folly comes a consequence against immediate intention and dictated by mind, whose ultimate purpose is to preserve the human race. How? By making certain that human history continues by repeating itself according to a certain fixed course of events. Thus the sexual relations between men and women give rise to matrimony, the institution of matrimony gives rise to cities, the struggle of plebeians gives rise to laws; people in conflict with laws give rise to tyranny; and tyranny leads finally to capitulation to foreign powers. Out of this last debasement a new cycle will begin, arising out of man's absolute degeneration in the wilderness.

Without mind there would be no history properly speaking, and without history of course humanity is impossible. Those things that make history possible—and Vico here as elsewhere is not afraid of tautology—are human institutions like matrimony, laws, nations. These institutions manifest an ironical stubbornness, which Vico calls mind, determined to keep man inside history and meaning; the irony is that irresistibly men act out "the uncontrollable mystery on the bestial floor," even while, just as irresistibly, mind illuminates the darkness by giving birth to sensible patterns, endowing man with a history that his fierce lusts seem otherwise determined to expend wastefully. Instead of unlimited copulation there is matrimony, instead of uninhibited autocracy there are laws and republics, and so forth.

All this is described by Vico throughout *The New Science* as something to be understood more or less immediately, that is, without the prejudiced mediations of Cartesian philosophy or Erasmian philology. For Vico claims to be speaking exactly about the realm of unadorned fact. What men do is what makes them men; what they know is what they have done. These seminal precepts resound everywhere in *The New Science*. Human history is human actuality is human activity is human knowledge. Methodologically *The New Science* adds to the equation the scholar's contribution: the scholar, that is Vico, discovers all these relationships by *recognizing* them, or to use a favorite Vichian term, by re-finding them (*ritrovare*). If at times we are bothered by Vico's habit of himself repeating the essential sketch of human history from pure bestiality, to moderate rationality, to over-refined intellectuality, to new barbarism, to a new beginning again; and if we question the neatness of the cycle imposed by Vico on the huge variety of human history, then we are forced to confront precisely what the cycle itself circumvents, the predicament of infinite variety and infinite senselessness. Take history as a reported dramatic sequence of dialectical stages, enacted and fabricated by an inconsistent, but persistent humanity, Vico seems to be saying, and you will equally avoid both the despair of seeing history as gratuitous occurrence and the boredom of seeing history as realizing a wholly foreordained blueprint. And never mind if epistemologically the status of repetition itself is uncertain: repetition is useful as a way of showing that history and actuality are all about human persistence, and not about divine originality.

It is most nearly true to say, I think, that whatever else it is, repetition for Vico is something that takes place inside actuality, as much inside human action in the realm of facts as inside the mind while surveying the realm of action. Indeed repetition connects reason with raw experience. First, on the level of meaning, experience accumulates meaning as the weight of past and similar experiences return. Men are always afraid of their fathers; they bury their dead; they invariably worship a divinity fashioned in their image. These repetitions are what human society is based on. Second, repetition contains experience in a way; repetition is the frame within which man represents himself to himself and for others. The primitive *pater familias* sets himself up as Jove does, repeating his imperiousness, ruler of a family he has created and which he must try to keep from overthrowing him. Finally, third, repetition restores the past to the scholar, illuminating his research by an inexhaustible constancy. "In the night of thick darkness enveloping the earliest antiquity, so remote from ourselves, there shines the eternal and never-failing light of a truth beyond all question: that the world of civil society has certainly been made by men, and that its principles are therefore to be found within the modifications of our own human mind." [2] For Vico then, whether as the beginning of sense, as representation, as archeological reconstruction, repetition is a principle of economy giving facts their historical factuality, and reality its existential sense. Certainly it is true that each repetition of a cycle or *ricorso* is generally the same as its predecessors; yet Vico is sensitive to the losses and gains, the differences, in short, within each repeating phase of the cycle.

Formally speaking, then, Vico's understanding and use of repetition bears resemblance to musical techniques of repetition, in particular those of the *cantus firmus* or of the chaconne, or to cite the most developed classical instance, Bach's *Goldberg Vari-*

[2] Vico, p. 96.

ations. By these devices a ground motif anchors the ornamental variations taking place above it. Despite the proliferation of changing rhythms, patterns, harmonies, the ground motif recurs throughout, as if to demonstrate its staying power and its capacity for endless elaboration. As Vico saw the phenomenon in human history, there is in these musical forms a tension between the contrariety, or eccentricity of the variation, and the constancy and asserted rationality of the *cantus firmus.* Nothing Vico could have said about mind's triumph over irrationality can equal the quiet triumph that occurs at the end of the *Goldberg Variations,* as the theme returns in its exact first form to close off and seal the aberrant variations it has generated. These uses of repetition conserve the field of activity; they give it its shape and identity, as Vico saw repetition confirming the essential facts of what he called gentile human history.

I use Vico's word "gentile" advisedly now. What we cannot describe formally in music, except by rather strained analogy, is Vico's notion of human history being generated, being produced and reproduced in the very way that men generate themselves by procreating and elaborating the species. Gentile history is the history of the *gens* and *gentes* who are generated naturally in time, and develop there; they are not created once and for all by a sacred power standing outside history. All of *The New Science* concerns this gentile process, and Vico's ideas about repetition are impregnated with it. His images for historical process are invariably biological and more, they are invariably paternal. The passage I quoted earlier is perfect evidence for the cast of Vico's imagination which grasped the progressive movement of the *corsi* and *ricorsi* as the relationship between parents and off-spring. Repetition therefore is gentile because genealogical; Vico's etymological punnings on the derivatives of *gens* obviously captivated him since they work not only as representations of how history derives intimately from human fertility but also how words repeat the process in the production of cognates out of radicals: *gens, gentes, gentile, genialis, genitor,* and so forth. Generally then Vico understands repetition as filiation but, as we shall soon see, filiation that is problematic, not mindlessly automatic.

Students of Vico have not, to my knowledge, made much of the filiative obsession in his historiography; and neither have they associated Vico's genealogical investigations with efforts, roughly contemporary with his, in natural history to study generation, reproduction, and heredity. In both fields, in Vico's study of historical experience and in the work say of Maupertuis and Buffon in natural history, taxonomy was a device for identifying phases through which living beings pass and re-pass but more important—as both Vico and Buffon were able to show— "life" was a category that transcended mere classification, had its own internal and self-reproducing organization, as well as a force that was transferred from one generation of parents to the next. The question of course was to answer how life was generated and how it reproduced itself, once, as both Vico and the late eighteenth-century naturalists agreed, life was no longer considered to be the result of a continuing divine intervention in the affairs of nature. Repetition for Vico and the eighteenth-century naturalists is the consequence of, and indeed can be identified with, physiological reproduction, how a species, for instance the human, perpetuates itself in historical time and space.

According to François Jacob in *La Logique du vivant* the notion of reproduction was itself born in the early eighteenth century as naturalists took account of animal capacity for the regeneration of amputated limbs. At first it was believed that the organism reproduced both itself and its lost somatic periphery because it was realizing a pre-existing blueprint, or plan, which was an ideal model fulfilled by the whole of nature. In time this notion was given up. Instead it appeared both to Maupertuis and Buffon (during the 1740s, roughly contemporary with the last years of Vico's life) that nature repeated or reproduced itself by virtue of a sufficient internal capacity, demonstrated in the organization of organic matter into assembled elements, for generating itself from within. When it came to showing that reproduction and regeneration invariably produced similarity (that is, repetition) Buffon's explanation was that heredity, the pressure on the offspring, was guided by memory. Reproduction was the process by which organized elements from one generation were transmitted into the next generation; since this process was clearly not random, and since filiation involved strong resemblance if not always actual repetition, both Buffon and Maupertuis postulated a faculty, memory, whose function it was to direct the transmission of generations. Thus the repetition of features was guaranteed into the next generation.[3]

Vico employs a strikingly similar notion. History, he said,

---

[3] François Jacob, *La Logique du vivant? Une Histoire de l'hérédité* (Paris: Gallimard, 1970), pp. 84–86.

issues from the mind, and what is mind but historical memory, capable of infinite articulation, modulation, change. Fundamentally, however, memory restrains mind; memory is all about an actuality that whether for primitive men or for the most refined modern philosopher remains essentially a human actuality. However much it may seem to change, it cannot ever be more or less than human. *The New Science* studied the structures of this immemorial actuality as it is transferred from primitive to modern man, or, as Vico saw in one of those startling observations that dot his work, primitive man literally fathers modern man, the latter recapitulating, in some ways repeating, the former. According to Vico, history is where nothing is ever lost. Whatever is, has both a prior and a later form, the two connected by what I called earlier a problematic filiation.

Vico's theory of repetition is more problematic and interesting than that of his contemporaries in natural history. Memory for them directed the transmission of generations, it enabled reproduction: it did not, however, cause it, nor did memory manifest itself except in space, that is as a physical presence of one object standing before another. The difference between Buffon and Lamarck was that the latter introduced a temporal dimension into heredity. Time, and not a sort of vast general natural space, connected living beings to each other, a common past history with succession, duration, the possiblity of perfected organization occurring through generation.[4] Heredity involved a genetic theory, not a passive memory. Generation involves struggle; this was the essence too of Vico's gentile

---

[4] Jacob, pp. 158–59.

history. With struggle, as between the generation of the fathers and of the sons, there is difference generated, as well of course as repetition. In other words Vico was aware that filiation from some point of view is recurrence, but from another, that of history as the form of human existence seen as a domain of its own, it is difference. Since he was a historian, the vacillation in Vico's thought about filiation between repetition or recurrence and difference really expressed vacillation between an interest in the unchanging, the universal, the constant, the repeatable on the one hand, and on the other an interest in the original, the revolutionary, the unique and contingent.

These remarks on Vico, and my brief allusions to the history of thought about generation and heredity, are intended to accentuate the centrality of ideas about repetition to speculations about temporal process, to the idea of human productivity, and importantly, to the thesis that time-bound human facts must in some way be regarded as repetitions of some prior presence or as differences from it. We must take note quickly here of how in recent literary critical theory this problematic of repetition and originality is treated—also genealogically—as the problem of influence between a paternal strong precursor and a filial latecomer. Naturally I refer to Harold Bloom's plot for poetic history. My interest is in maintaining that for literary theory, for Vico's gentile history, for natural history up to and including Darwin, it is natural to conceive the passing of time as *repeating* the very reproductive, and repetitive, course by which man engenders and re-engenders himself, or his offspring. According to Jacob, survival thus appears to be the survival of the best reproducers, the best repeaters. The family metaphor of filial engenderment when it is extended by Vico throughout the whole of human activity is called *poetic;* for men are men, he says, because they are makers, and what before everything else they make is themselves. Making is repeating; repeating is knowing because making. This is a genealogy of knowledge and of human presence.

I think it can easily be shown that narrative fiction during the European eighteenth and nineteenth centuries is based on the filial device of handing on a story through narrative telling; moreover that the generic plot situation of the novel is to repeat through variation the family scene by which human beings engender human duration in their action. If a novelistic heroine or hero has one task set above all the others it is to be different, so heavily do paternity and heredity—and routine—weigh upon them. To be novel is to be an original, that is a figure not repeating what most men perforce repeat, namely, the course of human life, father to son, father to son, generation after generation. Thus the novelistic character is, I think, conceived as a challenge to repetition, a rupture in the duty imposed on all men to breed and multiply, to create and recreate oneself unremittingly and repeatedly. In Emma Bovary's refusal to be the same kind of wife that her class and the French provinces require of her the filiative bonds of society are challenged. She is a character about whom it is possible for Flaubert to write because repetition, her feeling of boring, prosaic sameness, gives birth to difference, her desire to live romantically, and difference produces novelty, which is at once her distinction and affliction.

In speaking about the classical European realistic novel I find myself once again reverting to Vico's problematic citation of human history as a series of genealogical repetitive cycles. And yet, both Vico and Flaubert seem to employ the generative cycle of human time because and even though *within* it, located at its very core, is a basic antithesis which time exposes rather than resolves. This is what I mean: Vico's filiative sequence, fathers and mothers giving birth to offspring, thereafter engendering not only families but a struggle between the generations, produces two sorts of consequence. One is intentional: "men *mean* to justify their bestial lust and abandon their offspring." The other is involuntary: "and they inaugurate the chastity of marriage from which the families arise." Both consequences are included in the repetition of human history, yet between them, quite evidently, there is a significant rift. For, intentionally, in an unmediated and wholly natural way, filiation gives rise not only to conflict but is driven by a desire to exterminate what has been engendered, the abandonment of offspring. Unintentionally, however, the opposite takes place: marriage as an institution is established, offspring and parents become bound by it. The same rift between intentional sexual desire and an unintentional thwarting of it by institutions takes place in *Madame Bovary,* for instance. History in Vico's case, the very form of the novel in Flaubert's, is on the side of institutions preserving, transmitting, confirming not only the process of filiative repetition by which human presence is repeatedly perpetuated but in addition, those same institutions—for instance marriage, or community—protect filiation by instituting *affiliation,* that is, a joining together of people in a non-genealogical, non-procreative but *social* unity. What is historically important about marriage to Vico is not that it enables procreation; rather, since procreation takes place anyway naturally (and wastefully, at least by intention), marriage as an institution interjects sexual desire so that *affiliations,* other than purely filial ones, can take place.

The father's place therefore loses its unassailable eminence. The paternal and filial roles, necessary to each other as much in their natural concomitance as in their mutual hostility, seem to give rise to other relationships, affiliative ones, whose undoubted historical and factual presence in human society concerns historian, philosopher, social theorist, novelist, and poet. But an additional complication has crept in. You will have noticed of course that in speaking of the origin of affiliative relationships I used the somewhat dodgy explanation "to give rise to." This phrase avoids more common metaphors usually used, "to give birth to," or "the birth of" which, considering the antithesis between genealogical filiation and social affiliation I have been sketching, are metaphors I could not have used without explanation. Men give birth to; human beings are born. Is the same kind of description possible, and does it make as much sense in discussing social or literary phenomena? [5] Moreover, and this question is the truly relevant one, within the framework of *repeating* human gentile history what methods are there for dealing with the interdiction of paternal and filial sequences,

[5] Historians of science have evolved sophisticated techniques for reducing their dependence on the biological model; what they mean by "nascent moments" and "emergence phenomena" is highly special. See, for example, Gerald Holton, *Thematic Origins of Modern Thought: Kepler to Einstein* (Cambridge, Mass.: Harvard Univ. Press, 1975), and Ian Hacking, *The Emergence of Probability: A Philosophical Study of Early Ideas About Probability, Induction and Statistical Inference* (London: Cambridge Univ. Press, 1975).

what forms, what images, if *not* the generative, procreative ones
we would otherwise employ without second thought?

These are questions I should like now to try to investigate in
some specific instances. My perspective will remain the one I
sketched earlier in these remarks, in which repetition is an optic
employed (or employable) to discuss, portray, analyze the continuity, the perpetuity, and the *recurrency* of human history.
Among the most interesting and, I think, effective contemporary efforts to deal with the first appearance of something, say a
scientific discovery or the datable advent of an institution, are
Michel Foucault's archeological studies. The difference between
what he does in *La Naissance de la clinique, Surveiller et punir: La
Naissance de la prison,* and what is done in the history of ideas is
that Foucault is determined to show the accommodations of singular events to recurring, that is repeating, epistemological
structures he calls discourse and archive. He shows the triumph
of regularity and recurrency over irregularity and uniqueness: in
this he belongs in the tradition of Georges Canguilhem, and in
this country, of Thomas Kuhn. Yet as is evident by the two
titles I have just cited, Foucault is attracted by the procreative
metaphor without, it seems to me, adequately trying to recon-
cile his extraordinarily brilliant conceptual formulations with
these metaphors of biological reproduction. Lurking behind his
archeological terminology is for him an acceptable analogy between the engenderment of humans and of institutions. For
there is an unresolved tension in what Foucault writes not only
between uniqueness and repetition, but also between filation
and affiliation as instances of repetition.[6]

---

[6] In Foucault's *Surveiller et punir: La Naissance de la prison* (Paris: Gallimard,
1975) there is a quite remarkable account of the connection between ideas

In Foucault's case, as in the cases of Harold Bloom, Vico, the natural historians Maupertuis and Buffon—one could add a great many more names—there is consensus of a very general sort: that from about the middle of the eighteenth century the problem of change, while customarily represented in many fields as the generation, reproduction, or transmission of life from parent to offspring, is intruded upon by a force or forces troubling the continuity. In natual history written during the early nineteenth century—Cuvier's investigations are a case in point—such discontinuity is exemplified in the theory of geological disturbances. Similarly in the study of language, theories of linguistic origin such as Herder's or Rousseau's, which depict a first parent-man uttering the first parent word and thereafter siring language as we know it, are disturbed first by the newly learned unimaginable age of non-Western and non-Biblical languages, then by the discovery that linguistic history, so far as the modern researcher is concerned, cannot be described as moving in simple genealogical succession. In still a third field, biblical hermeneutics as Hans W. Frei has recently described it in *The Eclipse of Biblical Narrative,* the congruence between the New Testament biographies of Jesus and factual recurrences in Jesus' life, a congruence heretofore imagined as genealogical, is

---

about discipline (taken from the army, schools, and the monastic orders) and the rise of the modern penal institution in early nineteenth-century Europe. As an idea, therefore, penality is viewed as a correction of delinquency; punishment comes to be considered a *naturalization* of the physical brutality formerly administered to criminals. Prison society emerges then as a mock family, uniformly celibate and disciplined of course. Curiously, however, Foucault never remarks on the resemblance, just as he seems undecided as to whether the prison is a new institution or a redeployment of old (or analogous) elements.

definitely split apart by Strauss, Bauer, and others.[7] In short, it is only as a kind of metaphorical nostalgia for early faith that the generative terms can be made to apply to the world of scientifically observable facts. The paradox is that everywhere the search for origins and genetic explanations was fueled rather than stifled by the inapplicability of these explanations, except as wish-fulfilling metaphors.

Vico's prophetic vision foresaw the paradox and, as we shall see in a minute, adumbrated the alternatives to it. The idea of repetition increases in validity as a consequence of the divergences between genealogical metaphor and factual discovery that I have just listed. The repeating patterns of which human and natural existence seem to be composed gain credibility as their genetic origin loses it. Yet at the very center of human reality stands the fact of human continuity, which, if one were to observe it as a fact of historical continuity, is yoked to human generation. How does one connect this fact of repeating generation to the very compelling facts of natural, hermeneutical, and cultural dispersion, divergence, diversification? Obviously pressure is placed upon what is understood by repetition, and for the two alternatives that will culminate, on the one hand in Kierkegaard's *Repetition,* and on the other in Marx's *Eighteenth Brumaire of Louis Bonaparte,* Vico is again useful. Recall that he had envisaged one cycle ending in dissolution, from whence human remnants "like the phoenix . . . rise again." Call this regeneration, an act of supernatural will causing, and making desirable, repetition. This is one form of repetition. The other

[7] Hans W. Frei, *The Eclipse of Biblical Narrative: A Study in Eighteenth and Nineteenth Century Hermeneutics* (New Haven: Yale Univ. Press, 1974).

involves circumstances that Vico can spell out in great detail: the rise of civilization, its flourishing, debasement, final dissolution. Here we note a pattern of repeating action—human social and historical existence—characterized by a general debasement in the level of existence, from civility to barbarism. And this pattern, while on the surface appearing to follow a genealogical line of descent, is in fact guided by *inner laws* of development and regression, laws social and historical that contravene the power of direct generative continuity.

Kierkegaard's book *Repetition* exploits the first view of repetition, but, given the eccentricity of Kierkegaard's genius, it does so in ways that no one, not even Vico, could have predicted. Kierkegaard's focus, here as in *Fear and Trembling,* is not on the general notion of repetition but on its infinite particularity, its exceptionality. We must remember therefore that both the young man seeking a repetition of his first love and Abraham have it in common that mere filiality, that is any human relation as between a husband and a wife, or a father and a son, is neither ethically nor metaphysically enough. Repetition is not recollection, and it is not longing for something not there. Repetition is *"return,* conceived in a purely formal sense." [8] For the poet, as for the Knight of Faith, there is conflict between the self and the whole of existence, which is God. Such conflict is a losing one, since unable to conform, unable to speak, the lonely self is threatened with its own annihilation, even though it never relinquishes its hold upon reality. For repetition involves no giving up, but a self-possession carried to the point of no re-

[8] Sören Kierkegaard, *Repetition: An Essay in Experimental Psychology,* trans. Walter Lowrie (1941; rpt. New York: Harper & Row, 1964), pp. 88–89.

turn. Existence itself, represented by the beloved's marriage to
another or by the sudden availability of a ram for Abraham, ab-
solves the self "at the instant when he would as it were an-
nihilate himself." Therefore Abraham and the poet can repossess
the world, repeat the minute particulars of experience in it, return to reality with a "consciousness raised to the second power,
[which] is repetition." [9] Abraham has Isaac restored to him
again, and the poet in *Repetition* says: "I am again myself. This
self which another would not pick up from the road I possess
again. The discord in my nature is resolved, I am again unified.
The terrors which found support and nourishment in my pride
no longer enter in to distract and separate." [10]

It is no surprise that such a religious result, and with it a
sense "that existence which has been, now becomes," is difficult
to understand. Kierkegaard opposes this type of experience
therefore to Hegelian mediation, which unlike the abruptness of
detailed repetition instead winds reality in and out of categories
that rob it of the very factual immediacy Kierkegaard seems
anxious at all costs to preserve. Kierkegaard's own writing,
especially in the forms it utilizes, attempts to compensate for
the rupture between what has been and what now becomes. *Repetition,* for example, is constructed like a narrative by James or
Conrad, complete with frames and narrators surrounding a difficult to grasp action. Yet so strong even in Kierkegaard is the
genealogical and procreative metaphor his philosophy of repetition is designed to transcend, that at the end of the treatise he
describes himself, Constantine Constantius, as "a midwife in

---

[9] Kierkegaard, p. 135.   [10] Kierkegaard, p. 125.

relation to the child she has brought to birth. And such in fact is my position, for I have as it were brought him to birth, and therefore as the older person I do the talking." [11] Whereas the philosophy of repetition remains *affiliation,* the means used to describe it are, according to Kierkegaard himself, filiative. But the tension between the two views is permissible presumably because faith enables their joint tenure. Vico would call Kierkegaard a sacred historian committed to gentile methods.

Marx presents the alternative reading of repetition in one of the classic texts for our argument, *The Eighteenth Brumaire of Louis Bonaparte.* Its superb opening pages, as well as the 1869 Preface supplied for it by Marx, announce hostility: against the thesis that history takes place freely or at the whim of a self-born great man, against the emotions of confusion created by complex events, against the lack of discipline in methods of historical analysis based on superficial analogies. Everywhere Marx insists on the formula for which the work has become most famous, that all world-historical events occur twice, first as tragedy, then as farce. Repetition is debasement, but for Marx, unlike either the Swift of *The Polite Conversation* or the Flaubert of the *Dictionnaire des idées reçues,* debasement is not a function of seeing human society as a closed system of stupidly uttered clichés, but a consequence of a *methodological* theory of relationship between one event and another. Marx wishes to stay clear of positivism, vulgar determinism, and distracted hand-wringing or regret. If it is true that events of importance occur twice, then repetition is their spatial form; their aesthetic, po-

[11] Kierkegaard, p. 136.

litical, and temporal form, however, is different. But how is
this to be demonstrated?

   Standing behind Louis Bonaparte is not his father but his
uncle, the great emperor; just as before 1848 there is not 1847
but 1789, and before farce, tragedy, before the *Eighteenth Brumaire's* opening not merely everyone who wrote before Marx but
cardinally Hegel and Diderot. What installs these forcibly insti-
tuted precedents, Marx tells us in the 1869 Preface, is an occurrence within French literature, an occurrence little noticed outside France—and the whole of the *Eighteenth Brumaire* is a
forcible repetition of this occurrence in Marx's terms—namely,
a blow dealt the Napoleonic legend "by the weapons of historical research, criticism, satire and wit" (*"mit den Waffen der Ge-
schichtsforschung, der Kritik, der Satire und des Witzes"*).[12] For if
Napoleon III pretends that he is really Napoleon II, a direct descendant of the Emperor, it is the task of the historian to see the
facts as they are, that the son is really the nephew: Louis's
genealogical revision is thus set right polemically by Marx's,
and a French reality is universalized, Engels was later to say, for
scientific socialism. The *gen* in *legend,* a word related etymologi-
cally to *legere* and *logos,* bears only a *superficial* and misleading
relation to the *gen* either in *genitor* or in *genialis.* Marx therefore
corrects the egregious error fathered by the Napoleonic legend,
that a great man bears a son who in turn inherits his position.

---

[12] Marx, *Der Achtzehnt Brumaire des Louis Bonaparte* (Berlin: Dietz Verlag,
1947), p. 8. I have availed myself of the excellent new translation by Ben
Fowkes in Marx, *Surveys From Exile,* ed. David Fernbach (London: Pelican
Books, 1973); the passage quoted from the German above appears in the
Fowkes translation on page 144. Henceforth two page references, the English
first, will be given parenthetically in my text.

What Marx does in his own writing is to show that rewritten history can be re-rewritten, that one sort of repetition usurped by the nephew is but a parodied repetition of the filial relationship.

The importance of language and representation to Marx's method are crucial. Not only is his exploitation of every verbal device enough to make the *Eighteenth Brumaire* a masterpiece of intellectual literature; but Marx reflects in his language an understanding of the way in which language itself, while genealogically transmitted from generation to generation, is not simply a fact of biological heredity but a fact as well of parodically acquired identity:

> The revolution of 1848 knew no better than to parody at some points 1789 and at others the revolutionary traditions 1793–5. In the same way, the beginner who has learned a new language always retranslates it into his mother tongue: he can only be said to have appropriated the spirit of the new language and to be able to express himself in it freely when he can manipulate it without reference to the old, and when he forgets his original language while using the new one. (p. 147/15)

In language as in families, Marx implies, the past weighs heavily on the present, making more demands than providing help. The direct genealogical line is parenthood and filiation which, whether in language or in the family, will produce a disguised quasi-monstrous offspring, that is farce or debased language, rather than a handsome copy of the precursor or parent—unless the past is severely curtailed in its powers. But in the case of Napoleon III Marx perceives a whole series of pressures for fraudulence at work, all of them, like a play of mirrors, blossoming out of the motif of repetition. The father or mother imposing an imprint upon the child causes him to repeat the past; second, the nephew pretending to be a son; third, the clownish monster (referred to near the end of the tract) bursting forth untimely and unnaturally as fatherless embryo, in reality *without* true genealogical lineage; fourth, the representative man claiming to be of one class but actually forcing another class to accept him as its representative (as Marx says of this class of petty landowners: "They cannot represent themselves: they must be represented": *"sie können sich nicht vertreten, sie müssen vertreten werden"*—p. 239/117); fifth, all the unproductive segments of society—the thieves, brigands, courtesans, scoundrels, and so forth—beget this creature, even as the class he claims to be representing, the landowning peasantry whose very role in society is to be productive, in fact is silenced and forever destroyed by him. Is it any wonder then that Louis Bonaparte's exploitation of his uncle's legacy centers precisely, Marx says, on that article in the Napoleonic Code stipulating that "la recherche de la paternité est interdite"? (p. 239/117).

In other words, Louis Bonaparte legitimizes his usurpation by appeals to repetition in natural sequences. Marx, on the other hand, repeats the nephew's repetition and so deliberately goes *against* nature. In the *Eighteenth Brumaire* repetition is Marx's instrument for ensnaring the nephew in a manufactured world of analyzed reality. From the work's opening sentence, the celebrated citation from Hegel, Marx's method is to repeat in order to produce difference, not to validate Bonaparte's claims but to give facts by emending their apparent direction. Just as the pretended son turns into a clearly revealed nephew, so even Hegel, who had considered the repetition of an event as a strengthening and confirmation of its value, is cited and turned around. Marx's account of repetition shows nature being brought down from the level of natural fact to the level of counterfeit imitation. Stature, authority, force in the original sink through each repetition into material for the historian's scorn.

When Cromwell dissolved the Long Parliament, he went alone into its midst, drew out his watch so that it should not exist a minute beyond the time limit he had set, and drove out the members of parliament individually with jovial and humorous invective. Napoleon, though smaller than his model, at least went to the Council of the Five Hundred on 18 Brumaire and read out its sentence of death, albeit in an uneasy voice. The second Bonaparte, who, by the way, found himself in possession of an executive power very different from that of Cromwell or Napoleon, sought his model not in the annals of world history but in the annals of the Society of 10 December, in the annals of the criminal courts. (p. 232/117)

Only at the end of the work do we understand the true reversal of history and nature that Bonaparte has carried out, which Marx announces near the opening: "All that exists deserves to perish" ("*Alles, was besteht, ist wert, dass es zugrunde geht*") (p. 152/20).[13] To repeat a life is not to produce another life; it is to place death where life had been.

The *Eighteenth Brumaire* embodies the corrective transfer of

[13] There are some perceptive observations on Marx and Kierkegaard scattered through Gilles Deleuze, *Différence et répétition* (Paris: Presses Universitaires françaises, 1968).

vitality from the world of France in 1848, where it had been destroyed by death masking itself as life, to the pages of Marx's prose. Prose analysis captures and gives circumstantiality to Louis Bonaparte's masquerade as Napoleon's substitute, *"als den Ersatzmann Napoleons."* Marx's is neither a natural feat nor a miraculous assertion: it is an *affiliative* repetition. It portends a methodological revolution whereby, as in the natural and human sciences, the facts of nature are dissolved then reassembled polemically, as during the nineteenth century in either the museum, the laboratory, the classroom, or the library, facts are dissolved then assembled into units of didactic sense, perhaps more to illustrate human power to transform than to confirm nature. A parallel affiliative process takes place in philology, in fiction, in psychology, where repetition turns into an aspect of analytic or structural technique. Probably repetition is bound to move from *immediate* regrouping of experience to a more and more *mediated* reshaping and re-disposition of it, in which the disparity between one version and its repetition increases, since repetition cannot long escape the ironies it bears within it. For even as it takes place repetition raises the question, does repetition enhance or degrade a fact? But the question brings forth consciousness of two where there had been repose in one; and such knowledge of course, like procreation, cannot really be reversed. Thereafter the problems multiply. Naturally or not, filiatively or affiliatively, is the question.

The English Institute, 1975

REUBEN BROWER, 1908–1976

In Reuben Brower's death the English Institute lost a founder and one of its most active supporters; many of its members lost a great teacher and a good friend. His work, firmly grounded in the classics and the traditional disciplines, nevertheless continually sought out new directions and juxtapositions, and he had in recent years been increasingly concerned with the visual arts. This year's panel on Literature and the Visual Arts was one in which he expressed a particular interest. It therefore seemed to the speakers, several of whom had close personal associations with him, especially appropriate to dedicate that session, affectionately, sadly, gratefully, to his memory.

The Program

Friday, August 29, through Monday, September 1, 1975

I. BEN JONSON
   Directed by Jonas Barish, University of California, Berkeley
   Fri. 1:45 P.M.   "BEN. / JONSON": THE POET IN THE POEMS
                     Richard C. Newton, Temple University
   Sat. 9:30 A.M.   STRUCTURAL INTERPLAY IN JONSON'S DRAMA
                     Gabriele Jackson, Temple University
   Sat. 11:00 A.M.   JONSON AND THE MORALISTS
                     Ian Donaldson, Australian National University

II. REVALUATIONS: ARNOLD AND PATER AS CRITICS
    Directed by Robert Langbaum, University of Virginia
    Fri. 3:15 P.M.   ARNOLD THEN AND NOW: THE USE AND
                      ABUSE OF CRITICISM
                      Morris Dickstein, Queens College, City University of New York
    Sat. 1:45 P.M.   WALTER PATER: A PARTIAL PORTRAIT
                      J. Hillis Miller, Yale University
    Sat. 3:15 P.M.   ARNOLD, PATER, AND THE FUNCTION OF
                      CRITICISM
                      Christopher Ricks, University of Bristol; from October, 1975, University of Cambridge

III. THE LITERATURE OF FACT
     Directed by Angus Fletcher, City University of New York
     Sun. 9:30 A.M.   ON REPETITION
                      Edward Said, Columbia University
     Sun. 11:00 A.M. AFRICAN RITUAL AND WESTERN LITERATURE:
                      IS A COMPARATIVE SYMBOLOGY POSSIBLE?
                      Victor Turner, University of Chicago

Mon. 9:30 A.M.   HISTORY AND MYTH
Northrop Frye, Harvard University, 1974–1975; University of Toronto

Mon. 11:00 A.M.   THE FICTIONS OF FACTUAL REPRESENTATION
Hayden White, Wesleyan University

IV.   LITERATURE AND THE VISUAL ARTS
Directed by Stephen Orgel, Johns Hopkins University

Sun. 1:45 P.M.   DESCRIBE OR NARRATE? A PROBLEM IN REALISTIC REPRESENTATION
Svetlana Alpers, University of California, Berkeley

Sun. 3:45 P.M.   PRISON AND THE ARCHITECTURE OF MIND, A STUDY IN EIGHTEENTH-CENTURY AESTHETICS
John B. Bender, Stanford University

Mon. 1:45 P.M.   ALEXANDER RUNCIMAN AND THE MYTHOGRAPHIC WORLD OF HOMER AND OSSIAN
Nicholas T. Phillipson, University of Edinburgh

Mon. 3:15 P.M.   COMING TO LIFE: THE NATURE OF NARRATIVE IN FILM
William V. Nestrick, University of California, Berkeley

Registrants, 1975

Ruth M. Adams, Dartmouth; Luther Allison, Framingham State College; Paul Alpers, University of California, Berkeley; Svetlana Alpers, University of California, Berkeley; Renee Owen Amy, New York City; Hugh B. Andrews, Northern Michigan University; Jonathan Arac, Princeton; Nina Auerbach, Philadelphia; Henry Auster, University of Toronto

George W. Bahlke, Kirkland College; Sheridan Baker, University of Michigan; C. L. Barber, University of California, Santa Cruz; Dorothy K. Barber, University of Minnesota, Morris; Laird H. Barber, University of Minnesota, Morris; James E. Barcus, Houghton College; Jonas A. Barish, University of California, Berkeley; J. Robert Barth, S. J., University of Missouri; Bruce Bashford, SUNY at Stony Brook; Rosemarie Battaglia, Lincoln University; John E. Becker, Fairleigh Dickinson University, Teaneck; Millicent Bell, Boston University; John B. Bender, Stanford University; Charles Berger, Dartmouth; David Berndt, Boston University; Jerry M. Bernhard, Emmanuel College; Warner Berthoff, Harvard; John Thomas Bertrand, University of Virginia; Murray Biggs, M.I.T.; Richard Bizot, Jacksonville, Florida; John D. Boyd, S. J., Fordham University; Frank Brady, City University of New York; Leo Braudy, Columbia; Susan H. Brisman, Vassar College; Marianne Brock,

Mount Holyoke College; Leonora L. Brodwin, Freeport, New York; Barbara Brothers, Youngstown State University; Judith Gwyn Brown, New York City; Jerome H. Buckley, Harvard; Lawrence Buell, Oberlin College; Daniel Burke, F.S.C., La Salle College

Lila Chalpin, Massachusetts College of Art; Pradyumna S. Chauhan, Beaver College, Glenside; James L. Clifford, Columbia; Richard Cody, Amherst College; Douglas Cole, Northwestern University; Arthur N. Collins, SUNY at Albany; Claudette Kemper Columbus, Hobart and William Smith Colleges; Frederick W. Conner, University of Alabama, Birmingham; Sister Theresa Couture, Rivier College; G. Armour Craig, Amherst College; Martha Alden Craig, Wellesley College; Marion Cumpiano, University of Puerto Rico; Margot Cutter, Princeton University Press

Lewis M. Dabney, Yale University and University of Wyoming; Emily K. Dalgarno, Boston University; Ruth Danon, University of Connecticut; Sara deSaussure Davis, University of Alabama; Winifred M. Davis, Columbia University; Robert A. Day, City University of New York; Morris Dickstein, City University of New York; Muriel Dollar, Caldwell College; Charlotte F. Domke, Johnson State College; Stephen Donadio, Columbia University; E. Talbot Donaldson, Indiana University; Ian Donaldson, Australian National University; Sister Rose Bernard Donna, The College of Saint Rose; Anne Doyle, Mount Holyoke College

Scott Elledge, Cornell University; W. R. Elton, Graduate School, CUNY; Martha Winburn England, Queens College,

CUNY; David V. Erdman, SUNY at Stony Brook and N.Y. Public Library; Sister Marie Eugenie, Immaculata College; Lawrence G. Evans, Northwestern University

Frances C. Ferguson, The Johns Hopkins University; Andrew Fichter, Princeton; Stanley Fish, The Johns Hopkins University; Philip Fisher, Brandeis; Angus Fletcher, City University of New York; Edward G. Fletcher, The University of Texas; Ephim Fogel, Cornell University; Leslie D. Foster, Northern Michigan University; Winifred L. Frazer, University of Florida; Warren G. French, Indiana University and Purdue University; Albert B. Friedman, Claremont Graduate School; Northrop Frye, University of Toronto; Margaretta Fulton, Harvard University Press

Burdett Gardner, Monmouth College; Robert Garis, Wellesley College; Blanche Gelfant, Dartmouth College; Janet Gladden, Harvard University; Jonathan S. Goldberg, Temple University; A. C. Goodson, Michigan State University; Terry H. Grabar, Fitchburg State College; James Gray, Dalhousie University; Evelyn Barish Greenberger, Staten Island Community College; Robert A. Greene, University of Toronto; Basil Greenslade, University College, London; Allen Grossman, Lexington, Mass.; Christian C. Gruber, SUNY at Binghamton; James Guimond, Rider College; Allen Guttmann, Amherst College

Claire Hahn, Fordham University; Robert Hallwachs, Drexel University; Violet Beryl Halpert, Fairleigh Dickinson University; Richard C. Harrier, New York University; Victor Harris, Brandeis; Phillip Harth, University of Wisconsin; Geoffrey Hartman, Yale University; Britton J. Harwood, Miami University; Miriam M. Heffernan, Brooklyn College; Suzette Henke, University of Virginia; Judith S. Herz, Concordia University; Margaret R. Higonnet, University of Connecticut; James L. Hill, Michigan State University; William B. Hill, University of Scranton; Howard H. Hinkel, University of Missouri at Columbia; C. Fenno Hoffman, Jr., Rhode Island School of Design; Daniel Hoffman, University of Pennsylvania; Laurence B. Holland, Johns Hopkins University; Suzanne R. Hoover, Sudbury, Mass.; Vivien C. Hopkins, SUNY at Albany; Chaviva M. Hosek, Victoria College, University of Toronto; John W. Huntington, University of Rhode Island; Lawrence W. Hyman, Brooklyn College, CUNY; Virginia R. Hyman, Rutgers University; Samuel Hynes, Northwestern

Gabriele Jackson, Temple University; Barry Jacobs, Montclair State College; David K. Jeffrey, Auburn University

Marjorie R. Kaufman, Mount Holyoke College; Norman Kelvin, City College, CUNY; Arthur F. Kinney, University of Massachusetts; Rudolf Kirk, Rutgers University; Theodora J. Koob, Shippensburg State College; Harold R. Kramer, Middlesex Community College; Karen L. Kramer, University of Connecticut; Lawrence E. Kramer, University of Pennsylvania

Craig La Driere, Harvard University; Mary M. Lago, University of Missouri at Columbia; G. R. Lair, Delbarton School; Robert Langbaum, University of Virginia; Richard J. Larschan, Southeastern Massachusetts University; Penelope Laurans, Yale University; Lewis Leary, University of North Carolina; James Lehmann, Yale Graduate School; Nancy S. Leonard, University of Pennsylvania; Richard Levin, SUNY at Stony Brook; Amy Lezberg, University of Massachusetts; Lawrence Lipking, Princeton; A. Walton Litz, Princeton; Joseph R. Lovering, Canisius

Isabel G. MacCaffrey, Harvard; Bernard A. MacDonald, Brooklyn, Conn.; Hugh MacLean, SUNY at Albany; John McDiarmid, St. Anselm's College; Stuart Y. McDougal, University of Michigan; Thomas McFarland, CUNY; Jerome J. McGunn, University of Chicago; Terence J. McKenzie, U.S. Coast Guard Academy; Helen Marlborough, Franklin and Marshall College; Mary G. Mason, Emmanuel College; Howard Mayer, University of Connecticut; Donald C. Mell, Jr., University of Delaware; Elias F. Mengel, Jr., Washington, D.C.; Walter Michaels, Johns Hopkins University; John H. Middendorf, Columbia; J. Hillis Miller, Yale; Mary Ruth Miller, Tennessee Wesleyan College; Ronald B. Miller, Haverford College; Dolores Mirto, University of Maine

Ira B. Nadel, University of British Columbia; Rae Ann Nager, Houghton Library, Harvard; Eugene Paul Nassar, Utica College of Syracuse University; Lowry Nelson, Jr., Yale; John M. Nesselhof, Wells College; William Nestrick, University of California, Berkeley; Richard C. Newton, Temple University; Donald Noble, University of Alabama; Elisabeth Noel, St. Mary's College, Notre Dame; Gerda Norvig, Ben Gurion University, Israel

Martha A. O'Brien, University College, Dublin; Richard Ohmann, Wesleyan University; James Olney, North Carolina Central University; Stephen Orgel, The Johns Hopkins University; James M. Osborn, Yale; Charles A. Owen, Jr., University of Connecticut

Catherine Neal Parke, University of Missouri, Columbia; Coleman O. Parsons, CUNY; Roy Harvey Pearce, University of California, San Diego; Norman Holmes Pearson, Yale; N. T. Phillipson, Edinburgh University; Burton Pike, Queens College, CUNY; N. S. Poburko, Dalhousie University; Jonathan F. S. Post, Yale; Robert O. Preyer, Brandeis; Ruth Prigozy, Hofstra University; Jeffrey R. Prince, Northwestern University; Dennis J. Prindle, Ohio Wesleyan University; Alison Prindle, Otterbein College

Joan E. Reardon, Barat College; Donald H. Reiman, The Carl H. Pforzheimer Library; Christopher Ricks, Cambridge University; Joseph N. Riddel, University of California, Los Angeles; John R. Roberts, University of Missouri; Edgar V. Roberts, Herbert H. Lehman College; Nanette M. Roberts, Herbert H. Lehman College; Adrianne Roberts-Baytop, Douglas College, Rutgers University; Jeffrey C. Robinson, University of Colorado; Barbara J. Rogers, Ramapo College of New Jersey; Phillip Rogers, Queens University; Winslow Rogers, University of Missouri, St. Louis; Phyllis Rose, Wesleyan University; Roberta Russell, University of Connecticut

Edward W. Said, Columbia; Dorothy I. J. Samuel, Tennessee State University; Bonnie Sashin, Boston University; Helene Maria Schnabel, New York City; Joseph Leondar Schneidar, Curry College; H. T. Schultze, Dartmouth; Robert B. Shaw, Harvard; Patricia L. Skarda, Smith College; Jennie Skerl, Utica College of Syracuse University; Sr. Mary Francis Slattery, New York City; Alex Smith, University of Connecticut; Bruce R. Smith, Georgetown University; Carol Smith, Douglass College,

Rutgers University; John H. Smith, Brandeis University; Susan Sutton Smith, SUNY at Oneonta; Ida Mae Speeks, Fairfax County Public Schools; Robert E. Spiller, University of Pennsylvania; Susan Staves, Brandeis University; Milton R. Stern, University of Connecticut; Holly Stevens, Yale; John W. Stevenson, Converse College; Fred E. Stockholder, University of British Columbia; Albert Stone, Jr., Hellenic College; Gary Lee Stonum, Case Western Reserve; Rudolf F. Storch, Tufts University; Jean Sudrann, Mount Holyoke College; Maureen Sullivan, Marquette University; Stanley Sultan, Clark University; U. T. Miller Summers, Rochester Institute of Technology; Donald R. Swanson, Wright State University

David W. Tarbet, SUNY at Buffalo; Dennis Taylor, Boston College; Ruth Z. Temple, CUNY; Elizabeth Tenenbaum, Herbert Lehman College, CUNY; Chris J. Terry, St. Mary's University; Sr. Lucille Thibodeau, Rivier College; Mary Olive Thomas, Georgia State University; Robert D. Thornton, SUNY at New Paltz; William B. Todd, University of Texas; C. J. Trotman, Lincoln University; Marion Trousdale, University of Maryland; Lewis A. Turlish, Bates College; Victor Turner, University of Chicago

S. O. A. Ullmann, Union College

R. T. Van Arsdel, University of Puget Sound; Sara Van Den Berg, Davis, Cal.; James Venit, Queens College; Howard P. Vincent, Kent State University

Willis Wager, Boston University; Eugene M. Waith, Yale; Melissa G. Walker, Mercer University; Emily M. Wallace,

Philadelphia; Aileen Ward, New York University; Hayden Ward, West Virginia University; Rene Wellek, Yale; Barry Weller, The Johns Hopkins University; Hayden White, Wesleyan University; Robert O. White, Massachusetts College of Pharmacy; George Whiteside, York College, CUNY; Ellen Wiese, Harvard; Joseph J. Wiesenfarth, University of Wisconsin; James I. Wimsatt, University of North Carolina at Greensboro; W. K. Wimsatt, Yale; Hana Wirth-Nesher, Columbia; George Wolfe, University of Alabama; Michael Wood, Columbia University; Mildred Worthington, Bentley College

Curt R. Zimansky, University of Colorado